THE CLYDE

A Portrait of a River

MICHAEL MOSS

LOMOND

First published in Great Britain in 1997.
This edition published for
Lomond Books in 2002

Text and captions copyright © Michael Moss 1997, 2002
Photographs copyright: see page 160 for full acknowledgement

Design by The Hub Design Consultancy

British Library Cataloguing-in-Publication Data
A catalogue record for this book is available
on request from the British Library

ISBN 1 84204 046 4

Printed and bound in Spain by Book Print SL

FOR MICHAEL AND JUDITH

Contents

CLYDE SHIPBUILDING

The Clyde! – *it has been Glasgow's highway to fortune, as it is to so many of her people the highway home to the hills and the shore they came from. She made it herself what it is out of a shallow, narrow salmon stream, where cobbles precariously navigated; robbed it of its pellucid and pastoral charms, and in a century turned it, as has been aptly said, to 'a tide in the affairs of men'.*
Neil Munro **The Clyde 1907.**

Shipbuilding on the Clyde has a long history. The lower Clyde is a natural harbour and the gateway to the west coast. There are plenty of anchorages providing safe havens in a storm. The easiest way to get about the west of Scotland until very recently was by boat, because land journeys were often circuitous, arduous and, at times, dangerous. Journeys by sea were direct and there was a network of ferry routes and overland crossings linking the towns and villages up and down the west coast. For example, the route to the northwest from Glasgow was down the Clyde to Greenock and then by ferry to Lochgoilhead, a road journey over the hills to St Catherine's on Loch Fyne and then by ferry to Inveraray. It was also far easier to move goods by water than by road. Clearly, boats were needed to maintain and defend this transport system. Many of the vessels were simply large rowing boats but there were some larger sailing craft, known as gabbarts - heavily constructed beamy boats.

Little is known about early boat-building, but such evidence as survives suggests that ship-wrights moved around the coast constructing new vessels on the shore when they were needed. There were some more permanent yards in the lower Clyde ports of Dumbarton and Greenock and there was a Royal Dockyard at Cardross, where King Robert the Bruce built his great ships in the 1320s and which was still being used at the beginning of the 16th century by King James IV. Nearby Dumbarton, easily defended from the Castle Rock dominating the estuary, was used as a naval base and local shipbuilders were often contracted to construct vessels for the Royal fleet. When James IV visited the Western Isles in 1495, he had a ship repaired there and ordered 'a great row barge' and two smaller vessels. After his death at Flodden in 1513, part of his fleet was laid up in the harbour. Although the Clyde was of importance in controlling the west coast, it was strategically much less significant than the eastern seaboard, with its rich farm lands and extensive contacts with continental Europe. The Forth, the Tay and the Dee were the principal centres of shipbuilding in Scotland.

In contrast to these great east-coast navigable rivers, the Clyde, at the beginning of the 18th century, was a long shallow meandering stream, which could only be negotiated by very small shallow craft known as scows or cobbles, of about 20-30 tons' burthen. Goods destined for Paisley, Renfrew or Glasgow had to be unloaded at Greenock or Dumbarton before being taken upstream. In the 1630s, a local merchant called William Simpson built two wherries - at the Broomielaw beside the Clyde, and on the western outskirts of Glasgow - getting them down the river on a flood tide. Most Glasgow merchants, however, either had their ships constructed at Whitehaven or Maryport, on the Cumbrian coast, or purchased them from European builders.

The Scottish fishing industry began to develop in the early 18th century and, instead of nets being staked out from the shore, they began to be drawn behind open rowing boats. The whole of the western seaboard, particularly the Firth of Clyde itself, was rich in fishings, both herring and white fish. Demand for fish from the expanding towns in both Scotland and North-west England grew during the early 18th century and the industry became more commercial. The herring were taken to market in larger sailing ships, known as 'herring buses'. These ships began to be built in shipyards and the first recognisable shipbuilding company, John Scott & Sons of Greenock, was founded in 1711 to construct herring buses and other trading craft. By 1728, in Greenock alone, there were some 900 fishing boats operating during the season. To meet the demand for boats, other yards were soon established; for example, the Ritchie brothers opened a yard at Saltcoats in Ayrshire.

As Scotland's Atlantic trade developed following the Union of the Parliaments in 1707, so these early yards began to build larger ocean-going ships, mostly using timber imported from Wales and North America, as there was very little suitable oak available in Scotland. In 1718, the first ship for use on the Atlantic, weighing just 60 tons, was constructed at Crawfordsdyke, near Port Glasgow, but it was almost another 50 years before Peter Love launched the first square-rigged vessel to be built on the Clyde, appropriately named *Greenock*, in 1764. Two years earlier the Glasgow merchants had built a dry dock at Port Glasgow, which could take a vessel of 500 tons for careening and repair. Scott's of Greenock soon followed Love's example and began to win business from foreign owners. By the 1770s, Glasgow dominated the tobacco trade. With growing prosperity, there were calls for the deepening of the river, to allow larger vessels to come up to the city itself, and for the construction of a canal across Scotland to the Forth, to avoid the dangerous navigations round the north of Scotland and the south of England. The lengthy task of deepening the river began in the mid-1750s and, by the 1790s, ocean-going vessels of over 100 tons could travel up to Glasgow. The river continued to be deepened in the early 19th century, so that, by the late 1820s, over 700,000 tons of shipping was arriving at Glasgow's riverside quays each year. The Forth and Clyde Canal was started in 1768 and was finally completed in 1790, with a harbour in Glasgow at Port Dundas. These improvements encouraged the opening of shipyards on the upper reaches of the river. In 1818, John Barclay laid out a yard at Stobcross Pool, on the site of what is now the

Scottish Exhibition and Conference Centre and, in the 1820s, yards were opened further downstream, at Whiteinch.

Until the American War of Independence (1775–83), most of the ships used by Glasgow's prosperous tobacco and sugar merchants were built in America, where there was a plentiful supply of shipbuilding timber. When the war prevented them from ordering new tonnage in America, they began to buy from the local yards and quite soon a flourishing shipbuilding industry developed in the lower Clyde ports of Greenock, Port Glasgow and Dumbarton. The Minister of Greenock, writing in the *Statistical Account of Scotland* in the early 1790s, commented that, since the end of the war:

> Shipbuilding has gone on briskly in the ports of the Clyde. The largest merchant vessel ever built in Scotland was launched at Greenock about a year ago. She belongs to a company in the town, which has a contract with the Government for supplying the Royal Navy with masts from Nova Scotia, of which the company has already delivered at one of the King's yards 1,100 tons.

During the 1780s the Clyde was turning out about 6,000 tons of new vessels every year, which fell back in the mid-1790s to not much more than 3,000 tons. The principal centres of shipbuilding in Scotland continued to be on the east coast. Production began to grow in the early 19th century. More yards began to build for customers outside the west of Scotland and, with the end of the East India Company's monopoly in 1814, large East Indiamen began to be laid down, like the *Christian* by Scott's of Greenock for Stirling Gordon & Co in 1818.

In the late 18th century, Glasgow and its surrounding towns became important centres of the fast-developing textile industry, using waterpower and machinery imported from England. After James Watt's invention of the separate condenser (where steam was for the first time condensed outside the cylinder) and, later in the 1780s, the rotary engine, many textile mills began to be powered by steam. It was not long before local millwrights and engineers began to build steam engines, experimenting with them for the propulsion of ships. The first successful experiments were conducted by Patrick Miller of Dalswinton in the late 1780s, with the help of the engineer, William Symington. When Miller gave up his interest in steam propulsion, Symington carried on his experiments with his ship, the *Charlotte Dundas*, in 1801.

The first commercially viable steamboat, the *Comet*, was, however, built for a Dumbarton hotelier, Henry Bell, in 1812. With its hull built on the lower Clyde by John Wood of Port Glasgow, and its engines by John Robertson and boilers by David Napier, both Glasgow engineers, it set a pattern in steamboat construction which others quickly followed. Established wooden shipbuilders, mostly on the lower Clyde, built the hulls, and engineers, first in Glasgow and then in the other Clyde towns, supplied the machinery. Between 1812 and 1820, 42 steamships were completed on the river by such proven shipbuilding firms as Wood's of Port Glasgow, William Denny of Dumbarton, Scott's of Greenock and Fife's of Fairlie. Engines were supplied by firms like James Cook of Tradeston, near Glasgow, Duncan MacArthur and David Napier, both of Camlachie, to the east of the city, Charles Girdwood of Glasgow and Caird of Greenock. John and Charles Wood designed new hull forms for steamships abandoning the cod's head and mackerel tail commonly used in sailing ships.

David Napier became interested in designing and owning his own steamships, which he was convinced could safely be taken outside the sheltered waters of the Firth of Clyde. Before placing the order for his first vessel, the *Rob Roy*, completed by William Denny in 1818, he made voyages by sailing ship to Belfast to observe the action of the sea on the hull, and conducted experiments with a model to establish the most efficient hull shape:

> Having obtained a block of wood of the proportional length, breadth and depth I intended to build the *Rob Roy*, and having erected a framework close to the water of considerable elevation, at the top of which was a roller or drum for winding up a weight, the other end of the line being attached to the experimental block, I carefully noted the time the weight took to descend, dragging the block at the same time through the water, and continued fining the bow as long as there is any perceptible increase to the speed, always taking care to put the block on the scales each time I altered the shape, so as to keep the weight of the block the same, which block or model I gave to the shipbuilder to take off the lines for building the *Rob Roy*.

He was accompanied on the maiden voyage by his friend Charles McIntosh, the inventor of waterproof cloth, who was convinced they would be drowned attempting the first crossing of the Irish Sea in a steamboat. They survived and Napier went on to build a succession of steamers for the Irish Sea and Channel crossings.

One of the largest of these early steamship builders was James 'A'thing' Lang of Dumbarton – so called because he was willing to build anything. In 1811, he laid out the first privately owned dry docks on the river for 'repairing large vessels' and, in 1816, constructed the *Pestongee Bomagee* of 560 gross tons, one of the largest vessels to have been built on the river so far. He began steamship building in 1821, constructing the *Comet II* to replace the first, which had sunk. At the outset he used engines supplied by Duncan MacArthur and then, when MacArthur's business collapsed in 1822, he turned for his engines to David Napier and his cousin Robert, who also had works in Camlachie. Within ten years, he had become the most important builder of paddle steamers on the Clyde, having built 15 of the 59 vessels in service on the river in 1832. By this time, Scott's of Greenock were reckoned to have 'the most complete' yard on the Clyde and in 1826 Robert Steel & Co, also of Greenock, launched the *United Kingdom*, then 'the largest and most splendid steam vessel in the country'. Most yards were, however, small and were in business for only a few years, like the Littlemill yard near Bowling, operated by the well-known naval architect, Charles Wood, and George Mills from about 1834 to 1837.

During the 1820s, David and Robert Napier became the principal innovators in the design and construction of marine engines on the Clyde. Writing in 1841, the celebrated naval architect and engineer John Scott Russell declared unequivocally:

> From the commencement of steam navigation in Great Britain, no great strides appear to have been made until the year 1818, when Mr David Napier, the engineer, entered on the construction and improvement of steam navigation ... It is to Mr David Napier that Great Britain owes the establishment of deep sea communication by steam vessels, and of Post Office Steam Packets.

In 1821, David Napier laid out a large engine– and boilerworks at Lancefield on the Clyde, in the middle of Glasgow, near to where the Scottish Exhibition and Conference Centre now is. Alongside the works was a basin where ships could be brought up river to have their engines fitted, the engines being lifted on board with massive sheerlegs. Robert Napier took over David's Camlachie works, securing his first contract for water pipes for Glasgow Corporation, followed by a stationary steam engine for a textile mill in Dundee. Wishing to build marine engines like his cousin, he won an order in 1823 for the paddle steamer *Leven* from A'thing Lang. The engines, which incorporated several novel features, outlasted three hulls. Further orders were quickly placed with the firm. In the spring of 1827 Robert Napier spent time promoting his skill as an engine builder in London. This skill was confirmed later in the year when two steamers fitted with his engines won a race sponsored by the Northern Yacht Club. The race attracted the attention of Thomas Assheton Smith, who over the next twenty years ordered a series of innovative steam yachts from Napier. Following this success, Napier purchased the Camlachie works and the Vulcan Foundry, previously Duncan MacArthur's machine shop, which was not far from his cousin's Lancefield works.

Together David and Robert Napier made many improvements to the marine engine, culminating in the side-lever steeple engine of 1835, so called because of its shape. During the year, David Napier leased the now well-established Lancefield Foundry to Robert and moved to London, where he believed prospects for the shipbuilding industry to be better. Within two years the Bank of Scotland considered Robert's business 'to be very profitable' and his customers to be 'of the best description'. Over the next 20 years, the Lancefield Foundry acted as a kindergarten for the Clyde shipbuilding industry. Robert Napier and his foreman, David Elder, trained men such as Peter Denny and his son William Denny III, the brothers James and George Thomson, John Elder, Charles Randolph and William Pearce, all of whom became prominent shipbuilders later in the century.

Although the Clyde had enjoyed a lead in steamship-building in the 1810s, this was lost in the 1820s and 1830s as shipbuilders in other parts of Britain copied and improved on Henry Bell's example. It has been estimated that, between 1810 and 1819, over 67 per cent of all steamships constructed in the United Kingdom were built in Glasgow, but in the following two decades this fell to a little over 20 per cent. The Clyde began to recapture its dominant position in the next decade by the introduction from England of the new cost-saving technique of iron shipbuilding. The first iron shipyard on the Clyde was opened across the river from the Lancefield works in 1837 by Tod & McGregor, who had both worked for David Napier and had set up their own engineering firm in 1833. The venture was so successful that they laid out a larger yard at Meadowside, at the mouth of the River Kelvin in 1844. With plentiful local resources of coal and ironstone, the Clyde was better placed than any river in the United Kingdom to develop iron shipbuilding, and other iron

shipbuilding yards were soon opened, both on the south bank of the upper river, in Govan, and to the north, at Scotstoun. It was, however, the business acumen of Robert Napier that was to make the Clyde's reputation for iron shipbuilding.

To win contracts, Napier was often prepared to offer financial inducements or assistance. In 1834, he built the *Dundee* and the *Perth* for the Dundee, Perth & London Shipping Co, deliberately at a loss, so as to gain further orders. He justified this in a letter to Patrick Wallace in 1833:

> In getting up the first of these vessels, great care and attention would be necessary to gain the different objects in view and, in doing this, an extra expense may be incurred, but which may be avoided in all the other vessels.

When Samuel Cunard established his British and North American Steam Pachet Co. in 1839, Napier took a shareholding in the venture and in return secured orders for the first four vessels. Over the next 20 years Napier's built a series of larger and larger liners for Cunard, who in later life attributed the Line's achievement to the quality and reliability of Napier's first engines. His Cunarders included the *Persia* (1856), the first iron transatlantic steamer, and the *Scotia* (1862), the most powerful ocean paddle steamer ever built.

Napier's financial practices were adopted by many of his pupils when they came to manage their own enterprises. In 1866, Barclay Curle & Co became partners in the newly formed Liverpool–Hamburg Steamship Company and, three years later, were offered a stake in Donaldson Brothers' proposed new steamship line to trade between the Clyde and the River Plate. Peter Denny, who effectively controlled William Denny and Brothers of Dumbarton from 1854 until his death in 1896, invested heavily in the shipping companies that were customers of the yard, such as the Albion Shipping Company, the British and Burmese Steam Navigation Company and the Irrawaddy Flotilla Company. Over 30 per cent of his considerable wealth came from these investments and, between 1865 and 1914, Denny's built over 250 specialist craft for the Irrawaddy navigation. William Todd Lithgow, a partner in Russell & Co of Port Glasgow, which specialised in tramp ships, took shares in over 170 ships built by his firm between its foundation in 1874 and his death in 1911.

In 1841, Napier opened his own iron shipyard, also across the river from Lancefield, at Govan, launching his first ship, the *Vanguard*, in 1843. He recruited his cousin, the talented young naval architect, William Denny III, as his shipyard manager. Among his early hull contracts were the first three experimental iron steamers for the Admiralty. Despite the misgivings of marine underwriters at Lloyds of London, iron ships were an instant success in the passenger market;

although the price was higher, running costs were about 25 per cent less than for wooden hulls. Robert Napier sold his iron ships to those firms with whom he already had special relations either as an engineer or as a financier. By the 1860s, he had launched over 70 ships for customers, operating in nearly every passenger market throughout the world and had built ships for many different owners, including several foreign firms and navies. These included P & O, the Pacific Steam Navigation Co, Donald Currie & Co, and the British, Canadian, French, Turkish and Russian governments. He was the first shipbuilder on the Clyde to have some of his ships photographed for publicity purposes. In 1848 he also took over the bankrupt Parkhead Forge in the East End of Glasgow to secure supplies of wrought-iron plates and forgings for marine engines. Within five years, he had greatly enlarged the works, installing four large steam hammers, named *Chromis*, *Cyclops*, *Tubal* and *Vulcan*, and a very large vertical boring machine. He also invested in the Muirkirk Ironworks to ensure his supply of materials.

Perhaps the two most important firms to be established by Napier's employees were J & G Thomson and Randolph, Elder and Co. After working as an engineer in Manchester, Charles Randolph returned to Glasgow in 1834, to open a millwright's business in Centre Street, in partnership with his cousin Richard Cunliffe, a yarn merchant with contacts in the local textile trades, and John Elliott. The new firm soon won fame for the accuracy of its gear cutting and machining. In 1847, James and George Thomson set up as marine engineers at the Clyde Bank Foundry, Mavisbank and, in 1852, John Elder joined the now established millwrighting business of Randolph, Elliott and Co (the name being later changed to Randolph, Elder & Co), which wished to start building marine engines. Both firms quickly gained a reputation for the quality of their marine products.

Randolph, Elder & Co invented the marine compound engine, building the first in 1854 for the *Brandon*, of the London and Limerick Steam Ship Co. This engine, in which the steam passed through first a high-pressure and next a low-pressure cylinder, reduced the rate of coal consumed per indicated horsepower by about a third. With such a saving, it was ideally suited to the long sea-routes to West Africa, Australia, the West Indies and South America, especially down South America's long, coal-less Pacific coast. In the late 1850s, Randolph, Elder & Co installed compound engines in most of the Pacific Steam Navigation Co's fleet, with a startling effect on fuel consumption, which in the case of one vessel, the *Bogota*, was slashed from 38 hundredweight an hour to 19. The firm supplied the first compound engines to the Admiralty in 1863 for HMS *Constance*. She was tested in a race from Plymouth to Funchal in Madeira against HMS *Octavia* and HMS *Arethusa* which were of a similar tonnage to the *Constance*, but with simple engines.

When the *Constance* was within thirty miles of Funchal she was 130 [nautical miles] ahead of the *Octavia* and 200 [nautical miles] from the *Arethusa*. The engines of the latter two had to be stopped owing to the coal on board being nearly exhausted, and they finished the distance under canvas.

In 1877, Chief Engineer King of the United States Navy paid tribute to John Elder's tenacity in developing the compound engine, 'designing and constructing every year several sets, each more and more improved in design and detail'.

Both companies relied on family links in establishing their businesses. J & G Thomson opened a shipyard in Govan in 1851. Between then and 1872, out of a total production of 110 vessels, they built 42 ships for companies or individuals connected with G & J Burns. Their brother, Robert, had trained with this firm and was superintendent engineer with its sister business, Cunard and Co. When Randolph, Elder & Co began iron shipbuilding at a small yard in Govan in 1860, they built their first vessel, the *McGregor Laird*, for the African Royal Mail Co, in which John Elder's brother, Alexander, held a senior position. In 1868, with John Dempster, another employee, he founded Elder, Dempster & Co and the British and African Steam Navigation Co, in which Charles Randolph was one of the principal shareholders. From 1861 to 1874, Randolph, Elder & Co built 16 ships for these two lines. This pattern of building for tied customers remained common throughout the industry until the inter-war years.

During the American Civil War (1861-65), many Glaswegians sympathised with the Confederacy and helped finance the purchase and construction of fast steamships to break the blockade by the North of the Southern ports. Many of these orders were placed for the 'Emperor of China' by agents in London. Most of the shipyards on the river shared in the orders for blockade runners. William Simons & Co built the *Rothesay Castle*, while Elder's constructed, in five months, the *Falcon, Flamingo, Ptarmigan, Condor* and *Evelyn*, all fitted with compound engines achieving a mean trial speed of over 20 knots. The contract for the building of the *Pampero* by J & G Thomson caught the attention of the Glasgow Emancipation Society, which, as its name implies, supported the North. The Society intervened and the ship was arrested on her way down the river. The Stephen's-built *Shenandoah*, the first composite screw steamer designed to compete with the tea clippers, was fitted out as a commerce raider for the Confederacy, destroying 37 Northern vessels. The purchase of second-hand tonnage by the Confederacy fuelled demand for new tonnage. J & G Thomson built the *Iona II* in 1863 for David Hutcheson, to replace the *Iona I*, which had been converted as a blockade runner but sank in the Firth of Clyde after a collision on her way to America. As a result, the *Iona II* was sold to the Confederates and another vessel ordered, the *Iona III*.

By the late 1850s, the contribution of firms like J & G Thomson and Randolph, Elder & Co, had given the Clyde an unrivalled position as the most important centre of iron shipbuilding in Britain. Between 1856 and 1860, it is estimated that over 75 per cent of all iron ships constructed in the United Kingdom were built on the river and, despite the efforts of other shipbuilding rivers to fight back, the total remained at more than a third in the 1870s. To accommodate the increase in production, larger shipyards were laid out. Barclay, Curle & Co, founded in 1845 at Stobcross Pool in the centre of Glasgow, moved down the river to a larger yard in 1855, to allow the firm to compete for bigger vessels. In 1864, Randolph, Elder & Co moved to a new shipyard on a greenfield site at Fairfield, on the South Side of the river – 'having gone lower down the river than any of the other large Glasgow builders, Messrs Randolph & Elder have at Fairfield about as complete and convenient a ship-building establishment as any in the world.' This investment allowed the firm, which was renamed John Elder and Co at the same time, to dominate the Clyde industry. In 1869, the year of John Elder's death, the firm built 14 steamships and three sailing ships, totalling 25,235 tons, nearly double the production of any other Clyde yard. John Elder was held in such esteem that on the day of his funeral:

> The busy works south of the Clyde were shut, forge and hammer at rest and silent as the grave. The forests of masts along the river were draped in flags, lowered in sign of mourning. A very army of workmen, dressed like

gentlemen, followed his body column after column. Respectful crowds lined the streets as if gazing on the burial of a prince...

Growth in demand for iron ships encouraged new yards to be opened. In 1851 the Stephen family, who had been building wooden ships on the east coast of Scotland since the mid-18th century, opened an iron shipyard at Kelvinhaugh on the upper reaches of the Clyde in 1851, building their first iron steamer, *William McCormick*, in 1854. Threatened by competition from the Fairfield yard, Alexander Stephen & Sons, as the firm was now called, moved in 1869 to open parkland at Linthouse in Govan, next door to Fairfield and gave up building on the east coast altogether. Two years later, they added an engine works to the Linthouse yard. In 1861, their yard manager Charles Connell had left to set up his own shipyard at Scotstoun. A & J Inglis, on the other hand, had started out as marine engineers in 1847 at the Whitehall Foundry in Anderston, gaining a reputation for the quality and power of their engines. They began shipbuilding in 1862 at Pointhouse, across the River Kelvin from Tod & McGregor's Meadowside yard. One of their early vessels was the *Erl King*, the first ship to steam round the Cape of Good Hope to Shanghai.

With the decline of Robert Napier & Sons in the 1860s, it was J & G Thomson & Co rather than John Elder & Co, who assumed their mentor's mantle. George Thomson became sole partner on the retirement of his brother in 1863 and died in 1866 leaving the business in the hands of trustees but under the management of his eldest son, James Rodger Thomson. The following year, the Company built its first Blue Riband holder, the *Russia*, for Cunard, said to be 'the most beautiful that ever had been seen upon the ocean up to that time'. In confident mood, James R Thomson wished to expand the business:

> We have the early prospect of being called upon to tender for several large vessels mostly mail steamers of a large size, larger than anything we have hitherto built ... we are not, however, in our present yard in a position to tender for such vessels.

In 1871, they sold their Govan yard and moved downstream to a remote site at Dalmuir, on the north bank of the river, named Clydebank after the new yard. Their engineering and boiler works remained in the original Thomson's premises at Finnieston and Kelvinhaugh until 1881 to 1883, when new works were opened at Clydebank. As intended the move allowed Thomson's to build far larger vessels, constructing the 4,000-ton liners *Bothnia* and *Scythia* for Cunard, in 1873 and 1876. However the move coincided with a trade depression and Thomson's found it difficult to secure profitable contracts and were constantly in difficulties with their bankers.

After iron steamship-building began on the upper Clyde in the 1840s, many of the lower Clyde yards continued to build wooden sailing vessels for moving bulky goods around the coasts of Britain and elsewhere in the world. Some of the sailing craft they built were fast clipper ships for the tea trade. Until the 1850s, the clipper trade was dominated by American-built ships. In 1856, however, the *Lord of the Isles*, built by Scott's of Greenock three years earlier, 'beat two of the fastest rivals that had too long monopolised'. Ten years later the *Serica, Taeping*, and *Ariel*, all built by Steele's of Greenock, the *Taitsing*, built by Connell's and the Liverpool-built *Fiery Cross* took part in the most famous China tea clipper race. The race was almost neck and neck for the whole 16,000 miles from Foo-Chow to London and finished with *Serica, Taeping* and *Ariel* all docking on the same tide. The well-known *Cutty Sark*, now preserved at Greenwich, was built at Dumbarton in 1869 by the firm of Scott & Linton, which went bankrupt during its construction. Completed by Denny's, she never matched the speed of the earlier clippers. The Stephen's-built *Maulsden*, of the Dundee Clipper Line, made a legendary journey from Greenock to Queensland in just 70 days in the 1870s. In 1897, the four-masted barque *Benares*, built by Murray's of Port Glasgow, made a record-breaking voyage of 48 days between Cape Town and New York. Perhaps the finest testimony to a Clyde-built sailing ship is in the novel *The Shadow Line* by Joseph Conrad, in this description of going on board the *Otago*, an iron barque built by Stephen's some years earlier in 1869:

Her hull filled my eye with great content ... At first glance I saw that she was a high-class vessel, a harmonious creature in the lines of her fine body, in the proportioned tallness of her spars. Whatever her age and her history, she had preserved the stamp of her origin. She was one of those craft, which in virtue of her design and complete finish, will never look old. Amongst the companions moored to the bank, and all bigger than herself, she looked like a creature of high breed - an Arab steed in a string of carthorses ... That illusion of life and character which charms one in men's finest handiwork radiated from her.

Conrad, who had taken his master's ticket in 1884, settled in Britain and became a close friend of the Clyde shipbuilder, W T Lithgow.

Although iron and later, steel, replaced wood in hulls of sailing ships from the 1850s, steam propulsion was not adopted generally for cargo ships until the introduction of the triple expansion engine in the 1890s. Until then, steamships were more expensive to build and operate than the large sailing vessels designed to carry heavy cargoes. The most successful of the Clyde tramp builders was Russell & Co of Port Glasgow, founded in 1874. W T Lithgow, one of the partners, introduced standard designs and labour saving devices for working the sails in an effort to reduce costs. Between 1882 and 1892 the firm built 271 ships and a bigger tonnage than any other yard on the river. In 1891,

Russell & Co launched the highly experimental auxiliary five-masted barque, *Maria Rickmers*, of 3,800 gross tons – the largest sailing ship in the world – for R C Rickmer's of Bremerhaven. She was lost at sea shortly after delivery. By the late 1870s, only during recessions would an established steamship-builder compete for the construction of large sailing ships. In the mid-1890s, Russell's began building steam tramp ships and, by 1899, had finally abandoned sail. Other sailing ship builders either followed suit or, unable to re-equip their yards to build the larger steamships, gave up.

From the 1870s the yards on the Clyde began to specialise in certain types of vessels, partly as a consequence of the physical limitations of sites, and partly as a reflection of the familial and financial relationships between shipbuilders and shipowners. In the 1870s, William Simons of Renfrew, who had started as general shipbuilders in Greenock in 1818, were the leading designers and builders of dredgers and ancillary craft. Their neighbours at Renfrew, Lobnitz & Coulborn, later Lobnitz & Co, had a similar speciality. Fife's of Fairlie, originally builders of fishing boats and small steamships, became the best-known firm of specialist yacht designers in the world in the late 19th century, beginning with the *Stella* of 1848 and continuing with such famous yachts as *Cuckoo, Bloodhound and Foxhound*. This trend in specialisation became more marked as vessels became larger and more complex. The yards on the upper reaches of the Clyde, like Alexander Stephen & Sons, Barclay Curle & Co and Charles Connell & Co, which were capable of building the largest ships of the 1880s could not increase their capacity without moving. Such restrictions encouraged firms to reinforce their links with their major customers, offering them greater financial inducements and designing vessels to match the specific requirements of each trade. Barclay Curle & Co formed strong links with the Glasgow based British India Steam Navigation Co, while Caird's of Greenock was linked with British India's competitor, P & O, and Scott's of Greenock with the China Steam Navigation Co.

During the 1880s, the Fairfield works of John Elder & Co, under the able direction of William Pearce, who had been general manager of Robert Napier & Sons, was the most profitable of the Clyde yards. Between 1880 and 1888, the yard turned out no less than 108 vessels. This achievement was more a reflection of Pearce's willingness to invest heavily in the shipping companies for whom he built, rather than of the quality of his ships and engines. Indeed, three Atlantic liners built by Fairfield for the Guion Line, in which Pearce had a large interest, rolled heavily and were uncomfortable, depending for their speed on large compound engines. Although Fairfield's built the first triple expansion engine, in which the steam passes, as the name implies, through three cylinders, for the *Propontis* in 1874, it was not successful, as existing boilers could not safely produce steam at the required pressure. Other lines in which Pearce held big stakes were the New Zealand Shipping Co, the Isle of Man Steam Packet Co, and the Liverpool and Great Western Shipping Co. In 1887, he was co-founder of the Canadian Pacific Steam Ship Co (the precursor of the Canadian Pacific Line) and, between 1880 and 1885, built eleven ships on his own account at a cost of about £1.5 million, to secure a continuous flow of work in the yard. By contrast, the loss-making J & G Thomson, under the direction of the gifted naval architect John Biles, reduced the ratio of beams to length in an Atlantic liner from twelve to eight in the *Aurania* for Cunard in 1883, which made for a shorter and much more relaxed crossing. They also introduced improved hull design, based on test tank experiments, for the first time in the Atlantic liner *America* (1883) for the National Line. She was not only comfortable but fast and economic. In 1888-89, Thomson's completed two liners, the *City of Paris* and the *City of New York*, which, despite technical problems, were acclaimed for their comfort – 'fitted with a luxury unequalled at the time'. Nevertheless both ships lost money and, by the mid-1890s, the Thomson family had been forced out of the firm because of their poor management.

With the development of mild steel in the late 1870s, shipbuilders quickly abandoned wrought iron in favour of this new material which was lighter and could be rolled into much wider plates. This allowed for the construction of even larger vessels. In 1879 William Denny first used steel to build an ocean-going passenger vessel – the *Rotomahana* and, within five years, 45 per cent of launchings on the Clyde were steel ships. By 1889, this total had risen to over 97 per cent. The changeover from iron to steel necessitated extensive re-equipment of the yards, with bending rolls and cranes capable of handling the larger plates and sections. Mild steel, which was tougher than iron, made it possible to raise boiler pressure safely which, in turn, permitted A C Kirk of Robert Napier & Sons to re-introduce the triple expansion engine in 1881. This engine having three cylinders, was much more economic in service than the existing compound engine and soon became popular with owners, attracting more custom to the Clyde. The construction of larger steel ships demanded improved hull design. The work of William MacQuorn Rankine, Professor of Civil Engineering at the University of Glasgow, on the structural strength of hulls, and William Denny III on hull forms improved safety, reduced the cost of building, and enhanced operating efficiency. In 1884 with the help of the English naval architect Robert Froude, son of William Froude, Denny's built the first commercial ship test tank in the world at Dumbarton. It is now a branch of the Scottish Maritime Museum.

Although the output from Clyde shipyards expanded dramatically between 1870 and 1913 to reach a peak of over 5 million tons of ships, it would be misleading to suggest that the growth was consistently sustained. The industry was subject to periods of boom and slump. The marked effect of the trade cycle on the industry's output is a reflection of the direct relation of shipbuilding to world trade for, with the onset of a depression, freight rates fell and owners cancelled contracts for new tonnage. The shipbuilders reacted by reducing prices and by offering even more generous financial support. Wages were cut, often triggering industrial unrest in the yards. This combination of circumstances forced weaker firms out of business. Lawrence Hill, owner of the Inch yard at Port Glasgow, was driven out of business in 1870 with debts of over £27,000, covered by assets of £23,500. In September, 1878 in the trough of one of the worst depressions in the 19th century, J E Scott, owner of the Cartsdyke shipyard in Greenock, went bankrupt. He had begun shipbuilding in 1874 with a capital of £2,500, borrowed from friends. He had good returns in 1874 and 1875, but was in difficulty in 1876 through contracting to build hulls for three steamers, all of which were delayed by strikes and lockouts, caused by wage reductions. He made a loss on every vessel launched from the beginning of 1877 until the time of his failure in 1878. Such an experience was not uncommon. Even the large and prestigious firm of J & G Thomson continued to experience serious financial problems in the late 1880s, when trade had recovered.

From the mid-1880s, naval ships became a significant part of the output of the leading yards, such as Elder's (renamed the Fairfield Shipbuilding & Engineering Co when William Pearce entered Parliament in 1885), J & G Thomson and Scott's Shipbuilding & Engineering Co. Since the 1830s, the larger firms had occasionally been awarded Admiralty contracts, mostly the construction of marine engines. In 1839, Scott's had supplied the engines for the *Hecate* and the *Hecla*. Between 1837 and 1876, Robert Napier & Sons had built 30 hulls and 58 sets of engines for the Admiralty, and six hulls and 27 sets of engines for foreign navies, including HMS *Erebus* and HMS *Terror*, the first armoured monitors, in 1856, and HMS *Black Prince*, the second iron-clad British battleship, in 1862. Captain Erasmus Ommanney wrote in glowing terms in 1843 from Beirut of the engines built by Napier for HMS *Vesuvius* six years before:

> You will no doubt, and with very good reason call me a shabby fellow for not writing you since I have had the pleasure of being carried so far by a pair of your incomparable engines; but I trust it will be satisfactory to hear that they have done their duty well, and are now almost as efficient as when they left Glasgow. I am proud to think they have been no expense to Government for repairs since we have been on the station .... There has no vessel done her work equal to the Vesuvius; always been ready when wanted, never had a screw loose.

In 1878, John Elder & Co built HMS *Nelson* and her sister ship, HMS *Northampton*, ocean-cruising broadside armour-plate ships, 'fitted with twin-screws each to be driven by an independent pair of compound engines'. Under pressure from the press to bring British naval strength up to that of the French, the Government began to place more orders with private shipbuilders. Out of the first batch of contracts in 1884, J & G Thomson won orders for seven torpedo boat destroyers and, after the passing of the Naval Defence Act of 1889, built two first-class battleships, the *Ramilies* and the *Jupiter*. Between 1895 and 1901 Fairfield's completed 19 naval vessels of all descriptions and increasing power out of a total production of 40 ships.

The growth in the importance of naval shipbuilding for the bigger yards accelerated changes in the structure of the industry. Despite the naval orders allocated to Clyde yards, the most important commercial naval shipbuilders at the turn of the century were the armaments firms of Armstrong Whitworth and Vickers, with yards on the Tyne and at Barrow-in-Furness in Cumbria. Challenged by this competition, John Brown & Co, the Sheffield steelmakers, took over the ailing yard of J & G Thomson at Clydebank in 1899 to provide an outlet for their heavy forgings. Brown's at once embarked on an ambitious investment programme, laying out new berths, re-equipping and extending the engine works and building a test tank at an estimated cost of about £500,000. In the same year,

William Beardmore, the owner of the Parkhead Forge in the east of the city, which made armour plate, purchased the goodwill of Robert Napier & Sons with the intention of moving the yard downstream to new large purpose-built naval shipbuilding and engineering works at Dalmuir. These took five years to complete and cost over £1 million. Early in its construction, William Beardmore ran out of money and was forced to sell a controlling interest in his business to Vickers Sons & Maxim. This combination troubled John Brown's and the Fairfield Shipbuilding & Engineering Co, both of which depended increasingly on warship contracts for a large slice of their order book. During 1906–07 the two yards entered into an agreement with the Sheffield and Birkenhead steelmakers and shipbuilders, Cammell Laird, to form the Coventry Syndicate, to tender jointly for naval work and to build an ordnance factory at Coventry. In 1907, a much more powerful alliance was forged when John Brown's acquired a 50 per cent shareholding in the Belfast shipbuilders, Harland & Wolff, to create the largest shipbuilding group in the world. The purpose of this alliance was to give John Brown's entry to Harland & Wolff's group of prestigious customers for giant passenger liners, and Harland & Wolff access to John Brown's turbine technology and to cheap forgings. The marine turbine, a rotary engine driven by passing steam under pressure through blades attached to a spindle, had been developed in the northeast of England by

Sir Charles Parsons since the turn of the century and perfected for the propulsion of warships and large passenger vessels by John Brown's.

Beardmore's Dalmuir Naval Construction Works was inaugurated in 1906 and considered to contain 'probably the finest collection of modern machine tools' of any similar works in the United Kingdom. The new works covered about 90 acres and had a river frontage of nearly a mile. The main building berth was covered by a huge gantry, unique on the Clyde, with:

> On each side of the berth four jib travelling or walking cranes, capable of lifting 5 tons, and having an overhead reach of 30 feet .... Eight squads can be at work on a ship, each having a crane for dealing with material.

The fitting-out basin was reckoned to be the largest in the world and the boiler and engine works were considered to be, 'one of the finest yet constructed. The length is 720 feet and the width 323 feet, so that the area is nearly five and half acres.' At the same time, the Parkhead works had been equipped with the heavy machine tools needed to manufacture the largest naval guns.

The changes in ownership and connections of the Clyde yards at the turn of the century were accompanied by the arrival of a newcomer from London, the specialist warship builders Yarrow & Co. This firm had decided to move because space at their Thames-side site was limited, and wages and steel were cheaper in Glasgow. Their new yard, situated at Scotstoun, was constructed in less than twelve months. Six years later Harland & Wolff made a direct investment on the river by purchasing the London & Glasgow Engineering and Iron Shipbuilding Company, owners of the Middleton shipyard in Govan and the Lancefield Engine Works, which had once belonged to Robert Napier, across the river in Finnieston. The Middleton shipyard was to provide the company with additional capacity, while the Lancefield Engine Works was converted for the manufacture of the newly invented internal combustion diesel engine. Lord Pirrie, the chairman of Harland & Wolff, was enthusiastic about the potential of the marine diesel, which had been developed on the Continent, particularly in Germany and Denmark. He is reputed, while recuperating from a serious illness in 1912, on being shown over the new diesel-engine ship *Fiona*, to have exclaimed, 'The Future!' Pirrie outmanoeuvred Barclay Curle & Co to acquire the United Kingdom licence for the Danish Burmeister & Wain engines and in 1912 began building their diesels at Lancefield for installation in ships built by Harland & Wolff in Glasgow and Belfast. In 1913, the Tyne shipbuilders, Swan Hunter, acquired Barclay Curle & Co.

After the outbreak of the First World War in August 1914, the Admiralty began to place orders for new naval ships with established warship-builders and to divert supplies of steel away from merchant builders. As the war intensified, so orders were placed with other specialist builders such as Denny's and Lobnitz. All the yards awarded naval contracts were quickly working round the clock. Trampship-builders, like Russell & Co, who lacked naval or specialist experience, were left at a considerable disadvantage. There were also major labour difficulties, due to the large number of skilled men who had volunteered at the beginning of the war. The shipbuilders and the Government sought a solution to this problem by trying to persuade the trade unions to relax demarcation lines between different trades and to allow unskilled men, and women, to carry out some skilled jobs. This dilution of skills was bitterly resisted by the unions, who suspected that it would be difficult to reverse with the coming of peace. After a fierce struggle, dilution was eventually imposed in early 1916, allowing women to work on the shop floor in the shipyards for the first time.

By early 1917, with rapidly escalating losses of merchant ships, a merchant shipbuilding programme became an urgent priority. The young James Lithgow, a partner with his brother Henry in Russell & Co, was recalled from the Front to manage a new department of merchant shipbuilding. He pushed through a programme for constructing trampships to standard designs and for the extension of shipyards. Under this scheme, several Clyde yards increased their capacity by adding new berths and enlarging their engine works. To meet the greatly increased demand for steel, new steelworks were constructed. Lithgow's efforts were well rewarded with a huge rise in output. By the time of the armistice, the Clyde had built a total of 481 vessels since the outbreak of war. Of these, 47 had been built at Clydebank, 43 by Fairfield, 69 at Dalmuir, 33 by Scott's Shipbuilding & Engineering Co, 48 by Yarrow's and 46 by Denny's. By the end of the war, the capacity of the Clyde industry had increased by about a third. Fairfield's and Barclay Curle had built new yards and William Beardmore & Co had constructed enormous works for the production of munitions, aircraft and airships. Commenting on the firm's contribution to the war effort, Lord Weir, a Glasgow engineer and sometime Minister of Munitions, dubbed Sir William Beardmore a Field Marshal of Industry for his contribution to the war effort - 'It was sufficient for Sir William to know that the country needed something and he felt that he could make it. He made his plans, he produced what was wanted, he went ahead and did the work, and when it was done it was early enough then to talk about finance.' The shipbuilders optimistically assumed that all the additional capacity built during the war could be profitably employed in peacetime. Although some shipowners had warned that 'we may find it by no means easy fully to re-establish ourselves in our ordinary sphere of operations', the shipbuilders had some grounds for optimism: over 900 ships had been lost during the war and very few new merchant ships, particularly passenger liners, had been built.

The war had brought further concentration of the shipbuilding industry on the Clyde. Russell & Co of Port Glasgow, which changed its name to Lithgow's Ltd in 1918, continued a policy of acquisition started in 1912 by taking over the neighbouring yards of Robert Duncan & Co and William Hamilton Ltd, both of which built similar vessels. Harland & Wolff, either itself or through its association with the Royal Mail Shipping Group, purchased Caird & Co of Greenock, A & J Inglis of Pointhouse, D & W Henderson of Meadowside and Archibald MacMillan of Dumbarton. In 1919, on the death of Lady Pearce, widow of Sir William, Clarence Hatry's Northumberland Shipbuilding Group took control of the Fairfield yard.

Directly after the war, Harland & Wolff planned to rebuild all its yards and facilities on the Clyde with an investment of over £10 million. They also acquired David Colville & Sons, the Lanarkshire steelmakers. The development of their Caird yard at Greenock involved filling in the West Harbour and removing the North Parish Church to make way for six new building berths, two of which were to be over 750 feet long. The reconstruction of MacMillan's yard at Dumbarton required the town's gasworks to be moved to another site. The biggest project, however, was the construction of an enormous steel foundry – the Clyde Foundry in Helen Street, Govan, to make large high-quality steel castings for diesel engines. Sir William Beardmore, telling his managers, 'Transport's the thing,' authorised the investment of £400,000 on the extension of the Dalmuir engine works to make it possible to build large turbines, and £250,000 on the laying out of three new berths and associated plate-working sheds, for constructing tankers and tramp ships. John Brown's, Fairfield's and Stephen's on a more modest scale, all planned similar investments in their yards and marine engine works. Most of the other larger shipbuilders on the Clyde also formed similar liaisons with steelmakers immediately after the war. The Northumberland Shipbuilding Group took over the Lanarkshire Steel Company and, in 1920, William Beardmore & Co, despite its already substantial investment in steelmaking capacity, joined with Swan Hunter, Wigham, Richardson & Co, the Tyne shipbuilders and owners of Barclay Curle, to acquire the Glasgow Iron & Steel Co, which had a well-equipped works at Wishaw. During that year, Lithgow's also took over the Clydesdale works of James Dunlop & Co, and a syndicate comprising Alexander Stephen & Sons, Yarrow & Co, Scott's Shipbuilding & Engineering Co of Greenock, and the Campbeltown Shipbuilding Co, bought the Steel Company of Scotland.

At first it seemed that the shipbuilders' confident predictions about future prospects were justified. Order books were filled as shipowners sought to replace all types of tonnage lost during the war. Beardmore's alone received orders for eight ships, including four liners. However, by the opening months of 1921, it was evident that the economy was moving sharply into recession. Shipbuilders found it increasingly difficult to secure contracts for new vessels in a very dull market and some contracts were either cancelled or suspended. Sir William Beardmore, recently created Lord Invernairn, blamed the collapse of the market for new tonnage in 1921 on wartime wage rises and demanded reductions. At Clydebank Cunard delayed work on the *Franconia* and the *Alaunia*. By June 1922, it was reported, 'sheds are empty, and all the machines are standing idle.' Projects to re-equip yards and engine works were halted. As early as May 1920, Lord Pirrie of Harland & Wolff had imposed a temporary embargo on all new projects, with the exception of the Clyde Foundry. Two years later, he ordered the Dumbarton and Pointhouse yards to be closed down as soon as the vessels under construction had been completed. Disturbed by the suddenness and severity of the recession so soon after the war, the Government had taken action by passing the Trade Facilities Act in November 1921, which guaranteed loans for fixed capital projects, and was extended to include ships from 1922. Several large shipping companies and some shipyards, notably Harland & Wolff took advantage of this new source of funding, allowing work to resume on a number of ships early in 1923. The relief was only temporary and nothing could disguise the serious structural problems facing the whole shipbuilding industry, not just on the Clyde but throughout the country.

Faced with the collapse in demand, the shipbuilders found

their integration with steelmakers an embarrassment. Early in 1923, urgent talks were held between all the steelmaking companies in Scotland in an effort to find ground for common agreement to rationalise the industry. These talks came to nothing, as it soon became apparent that William Beardmore & Co, one of the principal instigators, was in serious financial difficulties. Beardmore's had never been really profitable since the opening of the Dalmuir works at the beginning of the century. With few orders for new ships or the company's other engineering products, Invernairn was forced to borrow heavily from his bankers. By 1926, Beardmore's overdraft ceiling had been reached and the banks refused to provide any more credit unless steps were taken to re-organise the enterprise. The accountant Sir William McLintock was called in to determine what could be done to shore up the business. His report revealed the seriousness of the company's position and called for radical solutions. When Invernairn failed to take action, a Committee of Investigation was appointed in the spring of 1927, with the power to impose a strategy for the company's survival. A new managing director was appointed and he began closing unprofitable units and, by early 1929, he was confident that the Dalmuir yard had a good chance of survival if demand for new tonnage strengthened during the year; but, if it did not, there was nothing that could prevent closure.

By this time many Scottish shipbuilding companies, along

with their competitors elsewhere in Britain, were in desperate trouble. Demand for new tonnage had remained at a very low level for all types of vessel since 1921 and the signing of the Washington Treaty in December of that year had reduced naval shipbuilding almost to nothing. Only months earlier Beardmore's and John Brown's had been promised orders for new super-battlecruisers, which were immediately withdrawn. In the six years after 1922, John Brown's tendered for 131 merchant ships; but won only 23 orders at rock-bottom prices. By 1925, it was reported that, at Clydebank, 'the East and West yard ironworks sheds [were] … absolutely empty and like a desert …. Business is at present so unsettled that it is exceedingly difficult to have even a semblance of continuity of work.' Clarence Hatry went bankrupt in 1924 and the Northumberland Shipbuilding Group was liquidated three years later, draining all the liquidity from Fairfield's and leaving the yard in a parlous position. After Lord Pirrie's death in 1924, it became evident that Harland & Wolff was hopelessly overextended and rationalisation was inevitable. However, the directors were reluctant to close any of the yards permanently.

At the end of April 1929, Sir James Lithgow and other representatives of the industry as a whole met the Governor of the Bank of England, Montagu Norman, to propose the formation of an association to close redundant yards, financed by a levy of 1 per cent on all new tonnage launched. Norman was enthusiastic and to manage the project National Shipbuilders Security Ltd (NSS) was established a year later. By this time, the Bank of England had become involved as the lender of last resort in the rationalisation of several armaments and shipbuilding groups including Beardmore's, now more or less bankrupt, which Norman unkindly rechristened Beardless. He immediately took the opportunity of negotiating the sale of the shipbuilding rights over the Dalmuir yard to NSS in September 1929. The yard closed in late 1930 after the completion of the *Pole Star* with a loss of 500 jobs. The engine works remained open but, in the very depressed market, it was impossible to secure orders and it, in turn, was sold to NSS in 1934 and closed down.

The formation of NSS coincided with the massive slump in world economy and rumours that the Royal Mail Group, which owned Harland & Wolff and its subsidiaries, was more or less insolvent. This cast a shadow over the efforts to rationalise the Scottish steel industry, which, by now, were about to bear fruit in the restructuring of the industry around David Colville & Sons. As Colville's was peripheral to the Royal Mail Group, those responsible for the rescue of the Group allowed the amalgamation to go ahead. Later, NSS was able to acquire from the Group the building rights for Caird's yard in Greenock, MacMillan's yard in Dumbarton, and D & W Henderson's yard at Meadowside. By 1937, NSS had succeeded in reducing capacity on the

Clyde by some 20 per cent: seven yards had been closed, two had been mothballed and three were working under restricted quotas.

These were years of crisis on the Clyde and in the British economy as a whole. By August 1930, all the berths at Clydebank were empty and it seemed likely that John Brown's might meet the same fate as Beardmore's. The company was saved by the confirmation of the order for Cunard's new giant liner, which had been awarded in May 1930. Even though the contract was not finalised until December, work had already begun, at John Brown's own expense, in strengthening the berth, installing a new ten-ton hammerhead crane and laying the keel. Work progressed quickly and, by the autumn of 1931, the hull of the giant liner, Ship No 534, had taken shape on the ways. However, work was halted on 12 December 1931 because the London financial markets refused to discount bills outstanding on the ship and Cunard refused to agree terms with the Government for additional funding. Three thousand men at the yard were laid off, leaving only about 500 foremen and apprentices to keep the yard open on a care-and-maintenance basis. The enormous, almost completed, hull of Ship No 534 on the ways, painted with red lead as a preservative, soon became a national symbol of the depression. In his book, *The Shipbuilders*, which portrays the problems of the Clyde industry in the early 1930s, George Blake described the hull as 'looming in its abandonment like a monument to the glory departed, as if shipbuilding man had tried to do too much and had been defeated by the mightiness of his own conception'. Confident that conditions would eventually improve, John Brown's took the opportunity during the closure of the yard, to install welding equipment and second-hand cranes from yards that were closing down. At the trough of the depression in 1933, the Clyde launched just under 50,000 tons of shipping, barely a fifth of its capacity, and unemployment in many towns on the river exceeded 25 per cent.

Work on Ship No 534 did not resume until April 1934, when Cunard reluctantly agreed to amalgamate with the White Star Line, in return for Government finance for the ship, and for a second super-liner, the *Queen Elizabeth*. The author H M Tomlinson visited Clydebank shortly after work resumed and later recorded:

> There is one thing concerning the great ship a passenger in her will never see, if he did not witness it at the right time. This liner, when she was but half-completed, when she was only becoming, was a portent, as if form were appearing in chaos, and one could partly see the future. As one would say of such a vision as Dante saw, she was awful. From an eyrie aloft, a man who was lost in her looked down past vague dark ledges to the hollow profound of midnight. He glanced nervously behind him, to see that he was safe. The gloom around was

reddish, for the steel walls had been ruddled. The metal alley-way muttered and rang with frightful sounds. A witness stood there impeded by baulks of timber and festoons of cables .... In the pit below there were glowings of forges, and distant midgets busy about the fires upon such cryptical duties as pertain to the pit. Overhead an automatic drill began careering, to an infernal uproar. That ceased, and its echoes sank as grumbles into numberless unseen steel caverns. Near there I spoke to one of the riveters. He was crouched over a deck, thrashing a red-hot tongue of metal which thrust up at him from below. His face was glowing. He got off his knees deliberately, stood up, straightened his back, balancing his hammer in his hand. He looked like an independent man, though he was small and spare, as are most Glasgow shipwrights. I questioned casually the economics of so vast a ship. He told me to take my economics to hell. 'I dinna ken whether she'll figure in dividents but she's a bonny investment for me, mister. Is it economy to let us rot, fathers who know the work, and sons wi' no chance to learn it?

These views poignantly summed up the feelings of countless families on the Clyde and other shipbuilding rivers, bewildered by the severity and length of the slump which had cost thousands of jobs in traditional industries. The resumption of work on the giant liner in 1934 was taken as a harbinger of recovery.

Indeed by the time the *Queen Mary* was launched in October 1934, the outlook for the Clyde yards was improving, following the Government's decision to re-arm in response to the threat posed by Hitler's Germany. Within 18 months, the Clydebank order book was full, with contracts for liners and two battleships, HMS *Duke of York* and HMS *Vanguard*. With the re-armament programme due to be completed by the autumn of 1938, shipbuilders were not enthusiastic about investing in new plant for the Admiralty work. They feared that they would be left with redundant capacity, as they had been after the war in 1919. When war was declared in 1939, all the Clyde yards passed under Government control for the duration of the hostilities. The naval building programme was accelerated and work on liners suspended. So as to allow the Clydebank yard to devote the whole of its capacity to naval construction, the *Queen Elizabeth*, which was still only half fitted out, was sent to the United States to be converted into a troopship. During the war, the character of naval warfare changed and more aircraft carriers, light cruisers, destroyers and corvettes were required for convoy and beach-head protection than large capital ships. As a result, building programmes were regularly changed, much to the frustration of the yard managers. Since, with the exception of a brief period in the spring of 1941, the Clyde was out of range of German bombers, a great deal of ship-repair work was transferred to the Clyde, putting even greater pressure on the yards. Beardmore's Dalmuir yard was re-opened for this purpose.

Although there were heavy bombing raids in May 1941 with serious loss of life, particularly at Clydebank, there was little damage to the yards. Throughout the war, the Clyde yards that specialised in building trampships were engaged in the construction and repair of standard ships, which, at the height of the Battle of the Atlantic, were being sunk nearly as fast as they could be built. In an effort to raise output, the Admiralty and the Department of Merchant Shipbuilding, led by Sir James Lithgow, concentrated on increasing productivity, using new methods of construction, like welding, rather than enlarging yards. Engineers with no experience of shipbuilding were also employed in fabricating simple hulls for landing craft and the floating structures used in the Mulberry harbour towed across the channel within days of the Allied landing. The Clyde's contribution to the war effort was crucial, with average annual launchings of almost 500,000 tons.

After the war, demand for all types of ship was strong. The shipbuilders, mindful of the depression that had followed the short-lived post-war boom in 1919 and fearful that their businesses might be nationalised, were reluctant to invest heavily in new facilities. There were other difficulties in seeking to re-equip: steel was in short supply and the Government imposed severe restrictions on materials for new building. When world demand showed no sign of slackening, yards began to plan new plant to meet strengthening competition from Japan, Germany and

Scandinavia. In making these decisions, several firms seriously misjudged the market in believing that demand for their traditional products would remain buoyant. The staple diet of the Clyde – passenger ships of all varieties – only proved such a satisfactory main course immediately after the war through wartime sinkings and the technical difficulties that delayed the introduction of cheap reliable air transport. Barclay, Curle & Co, Alexander Stephen & Sons, and Fairfield extensively re-equipped in the early 1960s, largely to meet markets that were to disappear within a few years. As a result, the firms failed: Barclay Curle closed its shipyard in 1965, Fairfield went into liquidation in the same year, and Alexander Stephen & Son's yard was dismantled in 1968.

The demise of the passenger ship market in the 1960s was accompanied by a change in world shipping practice. Up-river harbours were closed in favour of ports at river mouths and, consequently, the demand fell for dredgers, in which four Clyde yards specialised. At the same time, new roads and bridges replaced ferries, which had been built by the smaller Clyde yards since the 1840s. In 1958, the dredger-building firms of William Simons & Co and Lobnitz & Co, neighbours in Renfrew, amalgamated and were taken over a year later by G & J Weir, the Glasgow marine pump manufacturers, who, in turn, sold the goodwill to Alexander Stephen & Sons in 1964 and closed the yards. William Denny & Bros of Dumbarton, specialists in ferries, went into liquidation in 1962, after an abortive attempt to reconstruct as hovercraft builders. The following year, under pressure from the Government, Harland & Wolff withdrew from the Clyde to concentrate on their Queen's Island yard at Belfast. Their remaining yards on the Clyde were shut down, A & J Inglis at Pointhouse and D & W Henderson's repair facility at Meadowside in 1962, and Harland & Wolff Govan the following year.

Although closures were inevitable, neither the builders nor the Government were prepared for the crisis on the upper river in the mid-1960s. Desultory attempts had been made by the shipbuilders throughout the 1950s to find a solution by amalgamation. John Brown had made occasional overtures to Fairfield, and Lithgow had tried in turn to sell Fairfield to shipowning companies. Similarly the Stephen family had made overtures to other builders on the upper river. By 1962, the situation had become impossible, the majority of the yards on the upper Clyde were incurring substantial losses through fixed-price contracts, poor productivity and rising material costs. On the liquidation of Fairfield Shipbuilding & Engineering Co in 1965, Fairfield (Glasgow) Ltd was formed, to manage the shipyard, with Government backing and under the control of Iain Stewart. He was convinced that the shipbuilding industry was not managerially equipped to remain competitive, principally through bad labour relations, reinforced by lack of communications and a failure to introduce the production

techniques being evolved in the engineering industry. In Fairfield (Glasgow) Ltd he tried to correct both of these problems. With the first, he was partially successful, but the price that had to be paid in wages was high and only aggravated the problems of other yards by pushing up the wage rates generally on the river. The introduction of production engineering was fiercely criticised by other builders in the belief that shipbuilding could not be forced into the straitjacket of work measurement and standard time. Unfortunately, Iain Stewart did not have time to prove his case.

In 1967, the Geddes committee, condemning the industry for its short-sighted attitudes, recommended the amalgamation of all the surviving yards on the upper reaches: John Brown, Yarrow & Co, Charles Connell & Co, Alexander Stephen & Sons, and Fairfield, into Upper Clyde Shipbuilders Ltd. The amalgamation was pushed through in 1968 by the Labour Government, in the belief that Geddes and the Government knew best, and without taking the specialities of the individual firms into account. The engine works were split off and remained independent. John Brown and Fairfield, as large passenger-ship builders, themselves ill-assorted bedfellows, were quite unsuited to an amalgamation with Alexander Stephen & Sons, small passenger-ship builders, whose yard was anyway not viable, and Charles Connell & Co, traditionally tramp builders. Yarrow & Co, as naval specialists, were always the odd man out. Moreover, if Upper Clyde Shipbuilders Ltd was to have effected a long-term reconstruction of the industry on the Clyde, it required a fresh start. Unfortunately, several loss-making and very specialised contracts were carried forward, notably the liners *Kungsholm* and *Queen Elizabeth 2* and the cruiser HMS *Fiji*, all of which were late and massively overbudget, and failed to meet their specifications. John Brown's alone claimed to have lost well over £1 million on the *QE 2* contract. As a result of taking over these troubled contracts, UCS was unable to implement Geddes' recommendation to concentrate on building standard cargo ships on a production-line basis to meet certain specific target dates. The *QE 2*, for example, was not finally delivered until the spring of 1969. In the event, Yarrow & Co withdrew from Upper Clyde Shipbuilders in 1971 and the company was liquidated in 1972. The blaze of publicity surrounding the collapse of the company and the subsequent work-in forced Edward Heath's Government to abandon its 'lame duck' policy and provide a rescue package. The Fairfield and Connell yards were re-formed, with further generous Government subsidies, as Govan Shipbuilders Ltd, and the Clydebank yard sold to Marathon (UK) Ltd for building oil-exploration rigs, later passing to the French group, UIE. The Connell yard was subsequently closed. With hindsight, the whole UCS experiment was an expensive fiasco that cost the taxpayer almost £100 million, without even providing a solution to the problems of shipbuilding on the upper river, even in the medium term.

By contrast, the yards of the Lithgow group at Port Glasgow, Scott's Shipbuilding & Engineering Co at Greenock and Yarrow & Co were able to remain independent. Yarrow, on the formation of Yarrow Admiralty Research Department (YARD) in 1948–49, effectively tied up the naval market for destroyers and frigates, leaving all the other naval builders at a disadvantage. Lithgow's Kingston yard was reconstructed to build very large crude carriers and laid out to facilitate an efficient materials flow and to keep charges to a minimum. Although the group had acquired the engine works of John Kincaid & Co, Rankin & Blackmore and David Rowan & Co in the inter-war years, these companies had wisely been allowed to retain their autonomy. With the fall in demand, the firm was able to close David Rowan and Rankin & Blackmore without damaging the group as a whole. Kincaid's was left as the group's engine builders and maintained its competitiveness by strong management and a continuous programme of re-equipment. Scott's Shipbuilding & Engineering Co was better placed on the lower Clyde at Greenock than up-river builders and had, anyway, always effectively straddled the naval, passenger and cargo ship markets, by specialising in submarines and second- and third-rate liners, and by building oil tankers and general cargo ships. Following the recommendations of the Geddes committee, Lithgow and Scott's were obliged to amalgamate in 1967 as the Scott Lithgow group.

Over the next ten years, the world market for ships of all types deteriorated badly. Even Japan, which had taken Britain's place as the leading shipbuilding country in the 1960s, found it difficult to win custom. Demand for very large tankers, which had become popular after the closure of the Suez Canal, evaporated following the Yom Kippur War of 1974, as inflation bit deep and world oil consumption plummeted. The search for alternative sources of oil on the sea-bed created demand for totally new types of floating structure, met largely by the creation of new rig-building yards, operated by structural and civil engineers, rather than traditional shipbuilders. A number of rig-building yards were opened around the Scottish coast, for example at the remote Ardyne Point down the Firth of Clyde, by the civil engineering contractors, Sir Robert McAlpine & Sons. The Labour Government responded by nationalising the shipbuilding industry in 1977, the only conceivable way of retaining any semblance of an industry in the United Kingdom. The existing structure of the industry was retained under the umbrella of a holding company, British Shipbuilders Ltd. On the Clyde, Scott Lithgow was encouraged to diversify into the construction of large-production oil platforms, using the big slip designed to take large tankers. Three years later, in 1980, after an internal inquiry, British Shipbuilders was re-organised into five trading divisions:

Merchant Shipbuilding Division

Warship building Division

Engineering Division

Ship-repair Division

Offshore Division.

The remaining Clyde yards were placed in the following divisions:

COMPANY	DIVISION
Govan Shipbuilders	Merchant Shipbuilding
Ferguson-Ailsa Ltd	Merchant Shipbuilding
Yarrow Shipbuilders Ltd	Warship building
Scott Lithgow Ltd	Offshore

After the election of Mrs Thatcher's Conservative government in 1979, there was a move to privatise the profitable parts of the nationalised industry and reduce the enormous losses that were being clocked up by other sections. In 1985, Yarrow Shipbuilders Ltd, the specialist warship constructors, was acquired by GEC. The year before, when it became apparent that Scott Lithgow, which had attempted to diversify into oil-rig building, was in serious financial and technical difficulties, the business was sold in a rescue package to the Trafalgar House group. Its capacity has since been closed and there are plans to build houses on the site, demolishing what remains of the works. Govan Shipbuilders was taken over by the Finnish firm of Kvaerner, specialist ferry-builders. Ferguson-Ailsa, which concentrated on small offshore vessels and dredgers, was rationalised into one yard at Port Glasgow and later amalgamated with the North Devon firm, Appledore Shipbuilders Ltd.

The outlook for the Scottish industry was bleak. At the end of September 1986, the EC announced that, because of a further decline in world demand for new tonnage, a new directive on shipbuilding would be issued before the end of the year, which resulted in the closure of further yards in the United Kingdom (but not on the Clyde) and elsewhere in Europe. The fall in the oil price, due to over-supply, forced most oil companies and oil-rich countries to cut back production and exploration, leading to a famine in orders for exploration and production rigs with their associated support craft. Cuts in Government expenditure throughout the world, combined with the collapse of the Communist bloc, severely dented defence procurement, causing problems for naval warship builders. The three remaining Clyde yards, Kvaerner Govan, Yarrow's and Ferguson-Ailsa survived the long recession of the late 1980s and early 1990s by improving productivity, cutting costs and robustly marketing their range of specialist vessels. The UIE yard at Clydebank continues to fabricate offshore oil rigs. In the still-fragile market for new tonnage, the future of the surviving shipyards on the Clyde remains uncertain.

The glory of the Clyde as the world centre of shipbuilding has passed for ever. All that remains is evocative photographs of the achievement of the industry at the peak of its power.

PLACING AN ORDER

Ships have always been costly to build, perhaps one of the most expensive and risky investments. There was the ever-present danger of foundering in a gale, running on the rocks, being captured by privateers or simply sinking because of neglect or old age. However, because of the risks, they could also bring handsome profits for their investors. From earliest times, shares in ships were divided up into 64ths, which could be acquired either in single units or blocks. Even in modern times, ships have rarely belonged to one individual. However, they were often managed by one shareholder, who raised the necessary capital for their construction and supervised their operations. Many managers were partners in what were termed shipping lines, or companies that controlled several ships with different groups of shareholders. Sir William Burrell, the well known Glasgow shipowner, ran his business in this way. From the early 19th century, some steamship companies providing passenger-liner services were organised as chartered companies with a large number of shareholders, for example the British and North American Steam Packet Co – better known as Cunard & Co.

From the mid-18th century, the Clyde had a very large number of shipping companies working first in the home and Atlantic trades and later, throughout the world. Because there were few outlets for capital until the 20th century, many people with funds to invest were willing to take shares. Most ship managers depended for the bulk of their finance on their family and friends, but all invited those involved in the construction to take shares. The reason was quite simple: if the builder, the rigger, the sailmaker and the chandler were investors, they would take better care of the ship's construction. Similarly, the master of the new vessel would be asked to take shares so as to prevent him defrauding the owners when trading in distant waters. Shipbuilders also often took shares in the large liner companies who were their customers

Before a ship was ordered, the builder would need reassurance that the finances were in place, because he would need to fund the construction either from his own pocket or more commonly, by discounting 'bills of exchange'. These were, in effect, promises to pay a certain sum at a given date, together with the interest that had been gained. These financial arrangements demanded the trust and security of the close-knit commercial communities which typified the Clyde ports until very recently. Everyone knew each other and knew who was trust- and creditworthy and who was not.

While the finances were being assembled, the manager would negotiate a price for the design of a vessel suited to the intended trade, or the navigation of the part of the world intended for operation. Today, invitations to tender are issued to many yards throughout the world and the most competitive price accepted, but in the past many orders were placed with yards that had developed long associations with an individual shipping company and were themselves shareholders. William Denny of Dumbarton had close relations with the Irrawaddy Flotilla Co and built all their ships. Peter Denny, the senior partner of the firm for most of the second half of the 19th century, was also Chairman of the Flotilla Co. Scott's Shipbuilding and Engineering Company of Greenock had close links with the China Steam Navigation Co, in which they were large investors. There are many other examples of such close relationships. Prices were based on previous experience. Ships were either built at a fixed price or on a cost-plus basis. In either case, accurate records had to be maintained of all the materials and labour used on each contract. The archives of all the Clyde shipbuilders contain tender books and detailed estimates for new tonnage.

Contracts, even as late as the 1950s, could be very simple-just a hastily written note agreeing to the construction of a ship with certain features and at a certain price. After the contract had been agreed, detailed design work would be undertaken to meet the owner's specifications. When the layout of the ship had been agreed, a vast number of large-scale full-size detailed drawings had to be produced for use in the yard during construction. Even simple vessels like sailing ships involved a very-large number of components and different types of materials. Many of these had to be ordered from sub-contractors before work began.

The drawing office at William Beardmore's Naval Construction Works at Dalmuir in 1905 with draughtsmen hard at work. Ship drawings were often very large, sometimes over 20 feet long. The drawing office and the counting house were at the heart of every shipyard. It was there that ships were designed and costed. Most yard managers had been trained at some time in the drawing office.

Making a half model of the hull of the Cunard liner *Aquitania* for accurately calculating the dimensions of individual plates and the alignment of portholes and doors.

The mould loft at the Dalmuir Naval Construction Works. The lines of a ship have been drawn out on the floor and wooden templates made up so that frames and plates can be made to the correct shape.

Drawing out the shape of the hull of the *Aquitania* on marble tables in the mould loft at the Clydebank yard in 1911. The hull form of the *Aquitania* is reckoned to be one of the most superb of the Atlantic liners of the period.

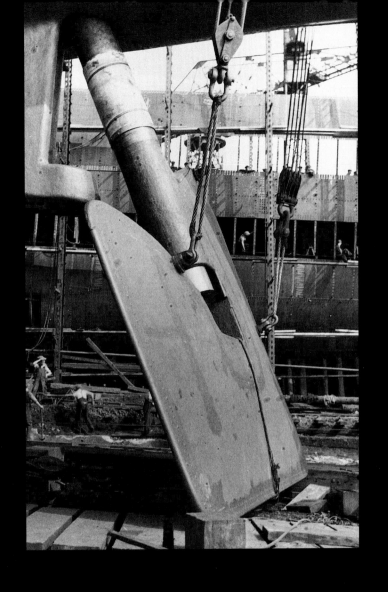

ON THE WAYS

Until recently, all ships were usually built on sloping ground beside the river or the sea. Early on, construction slips were very simple, often timbers laid on the foreshore to hold the weight of the ship. They were usually temporary, designed to build only one or two vessels. When shipbuilding became established along the length of the Clyde in the late 18th century and ships became heavier, much stronger ways were set out with wooden piling for support. The remains of some of these ways can still be seen on the banks of the river at low tide. With the beginning of steam and later iron shipbuilding, the yards became established and more elaborate. However, until the 1870s there were few gantry cranes. Most of the heavy lifting was done with temporary, simple, Scotch pole derrick cranes placed on the hull of the new ship.

The first task in building a ship was to lay off the lines to their actual size in a mould loft. When this had been done, wooden templates were made to show the shape of the frames and timbers or plates. These were laid out on a scrieve board, a large metal platform with a gridiron of holes. Steel pegs were placed in the holes to give an outline of each frame, which was made by hammering heated bars of iron or steel up to the pegs. Plates were shaped using bending machines in sheds beside the building ways. Frames and plates were then carried out to the ways on bogeys to be fitted into place.

While this work was being done, the ways were prepared by building a wooden slip which would slide into the water when the hull had been completed. This was a skilled task, particularly when ships became very large, towards the end of the 19th century. The builder could not afford the embarrassment of a ship accidentally launching itself or sticking on the ways. To take the weight during construction, keel blocks and shore and bilge blocks were placed just above the sliding ways. When these were in place, the keel was laid. It was essential that the keel was perfectly straight otherwise the ship would be difficult to manoeuvre in service. For naval vessels, keel laying was an important event with distinguished guests present, because it triggered the first progress payment.

After the keel was laid, cross-members were fitted to form the floor or bottom of the ship, which was plated to give strength. In large vessels, particularly naval ships, the tops of the floor were also plated to form what was known as a double bottom. While this work was being finished, the frames of the ships were put in place and braced by longitudinal frames known as stringers. At either end of the ship, the stem and stern frames were attached. These were single forgings or castings, bought in from specialist suppliers, like William Beardmore & Co of Parkhead. The stern frame provided support for the rudder mounting and, in screw ships, for the propeller drive shafts. The deck and bulkhead beams were then added and the whole ship plated. Before they were taken to the ways, holes to take the rivets were drilled in all the components. These had to be placed very accurately; otherwise the beams and plates would simply not fit together.

In the early days of wooden shipbuilding, the frame of the ship was made up in much the same way. The wooden beams and planks were shaped using heated sandboxes and held in place using enormous wrought-iron bolts and copper nails. Iron and steel plates were held together using rivets - short lengths of steel with a round head. They were heated by a boy in a small furnace, who then threw them to the riveter. They were driven into the hole and held up by the 'hauder-on' using a dolly – a massive lump of metal while the riveter hammered over the end of the rivet to close the joint. This was physically very demanding work and the noise was deafening. The sound of riveters working could be heard along the whole length of the river. Riveting teams were paid piece rates for the number of rivets they could close up in an hour. Some teams could get through several hundred rivets in a day. In the late 19th century, portable hydraulic riveting machines were introduced. Since the Second World War, welding has replaced riveting universally.

Sailing ships were completed on the ways and were sometimes launched fully provisioned, ready to leave for their trials. From almost the beginning of steamship-building, vessels were launched before the machinery was fitted, because the weight would distort the hull when the ship entered the water. In screw vessels, the propellers and shafts were installed, but not the engines.

Strengthening the ways at the Clydebank yard before laying the keel of the Cunarder *Aquitania* in 1911.

Laying the keel plate (the backbone) of the *Aquitania* in 1911. A hydraulic riveting machine is being used to attach the bottom plates.

Frames being bent in the enormous platers' shed at the Dalmuir Naval Construction Works in 1906. The wooden templates for the frames can been seen stacked against the wall in the background.

Plates being marked for bending, cutting and drilling at the Dalmuir works in 1906. The wooden floor on which the work is being done had to be perfectly flat.

The Glen shipyard of John Reid & Co of Port Glasgow, with five ships at various stages of construction, in the 1880s. No cranes for lifting heavy material on to the hulls seem to have been used. The ends of the sliding ways, protected by a simple cofferdam, are clearly visible on the foreshore. This firm had its origins in the 1780s, when John Wood began shipbuilding at Rue End in Greenock. The yard moved to Port Glasgow in 1811. John Reid, a nephew of John Wood, became a partner in the 1830s and took over the business in the early 1850s. The yard moved to Whiteinch on the upper Clyde in 1890, and closed in 1910.

A magnificent view of the other end of the ways at John Reid's Glen yard. The vessel in the centre is almost ready for launching. The hull has been painted, the figurehead has been gilded and the riggers are completing their work. The ramp at the left-hand side of the ship was used to take all the heavy materials on board.

Bending frames at Clydebank in 1886, to make up the shape of the bottom of a liner. This was skilled work as each frame had to be in perfect alignment. An error at this stage of construction would have been very costly.

The inner bottom of the liner *City of New York* taking shape on the ways, with the first ribs in place in the foreground in 1886.

Plating the inner bottom of the *City of New York* at the Clydebank yard in 1887. The 'hauder-on' had to work inside the double bottom holding the rivet in place for the riveter to knock up or, in this case, down.

Hydraulic riveters at work on the upper strakes of a vessel in 1914. The use of hydraulic riveting machines greatly accelerated the pace of work on the straightforward sections, such as this, of larger vessels.

Fitting the rudder on the King George V class battleship, HMS *Duke of York*, in 1941. The rudder and associated steering gear were a vital part of any ship, particularly warships, which often had to manoeuvre at high speed. Damage to the steering gear by a lucky hit from the cruiser HMS *Norfolk* spelt the end of the German battle cruiser *Bismarck*, which the *Duke of York* helped to sink in May 1941.

THE LAUNCH

The launch of a new ship has always been an occasion. Weeks before the date of the launch the ways had to be prepared. The scaffolding surrounding the hull was gradually removed and the bow and stern supported by wooden poppets designed to hold the weight of the ship as she entered the water. The sliding ways themselves had to be greased so that the ship would slide gracefully into the water. All the wooden keel blocks that supported the ship had to be knocked away, so that the hull could rest on the sliding ways until it was only held in place by a series of pins that were withdrawn at the moment of launch. To prevent the ship plunging uncontrolled into the water, huge drag chains were attached to slow the momentum. This was skilled work. If the drag chains were too heavy, the ship would not move and, if they were too light, she might run into the opposite bank of the river, particularly on the upper reaches.

A launch had to take place at high tide and for very large ships, like the *Queen Mary* or *Queen Elizabeth*, at times of unusually high spring tides. There was a ceremony for the launch of many large vessels with representatives of the owners, the builders and the sub-contractors present to witness a lady name the ship by breaking a bottle of champagne over the bows. In the early days, ships were encouraged to start moving down the ways by shipyard workers swinging a great bulk of *lignum vitae* against the bow end of the slip. Later this was replaced by a hydraulic ram, operated from the launching platform. Directly the ship entered the water, it was brought under control by waiting tugs and towed to the fitting-out basin to be completed.

Knocking out the props that support HMS *Hood* on the ways, before her launch in August 1918. This was always a poignant moment, signalling the end of a large contract. Shipbuilding has always been a cyclical industry and, if a launch coincided with a recession, many shipwrights could find themselves without work until trade picked up. Most craftsmen moved freely between yards in search of work, only the foremen were salaried and even they could be laid off during a serious depression.

The huge poppet fixed to the hull that supported the bow of the giant battle cruiser HMS *Hood* during her launch in August 1918. The enormous weight of capital ships required the ways to be well-strengthened. The launch of the *Hood* was delayed so that more armour could be incorporated in the design following the explosion of similarly designed battle cruisers during the Battle of Jutland in 1916.

The morning of the launch of the Atlantic liner *City of New York* in 1887. At the time this was the largest liner yet to be constructed and many innovations had been incorporated in her design – not least twin-screw propellers. With any novel vessel of this size, there is always the danger of a serious mishap.

The launch party for the *Foyers* at the yard of Scott's of Bowling in 1904. The *Foyers* was ordered by Paton & Hendry of Glasgow, who operated seven coasters under their own name and a further eleven vessels through the Glasgow Steam Coasters Co. In addition to shipowning, they also acted as ship-brokers, buying and selling second-hand tonnage.

The launch of the ferry *Dee-Why* from Napier & Miller's Old Kilpatrick yard in 1927, and the completed ship on trial. The *Dee-Why* was built for the Port Jackson & Manly Steam Ship Co of Sydney, New South Wales, Australia, for their Sydney–Manly service. Napier & Miller, like many of the smaller yards, did not have their own engine works and the engines were supplied by D & W Henderson of Meadowside

A bow view of Ship No 736, *Queen Elizabeth 2*, shortly before her launch by Queen Elizabeth in 1967. This was the last great liner to be built in Britain. Her construction showed up all too clearly the deep-seated management and labour relations problems in the Clyde's traditional heavy industries. There were regular disputes, delivery was months late and much of the workmanship was not of the same quality as in the heyday of Clyde-built liners.

The spectacle of a launch as the drag chains are torn down the berth – *British Judge*, an oil tanker for British Petroleum, enters the river at Clydebank in 1958. The two white strips in the centre are the greased launching ways.

The building of the hull of a ship is a difficult enough task but the fitting-out of a large liner or naval vessel is very complex, involving a bewildering range of skills and trades. It was the ability to fit out vessels to a very high standard that made the reputation of the Clyde as a centre of shipbuilding in the 19th century.

The engines and boilers had to be installed and connected to the drive shafts. The larger Clyde shipyards had their own engine and boiler works, building high-performance propelling machinery, often to advanced designs. Many of the smaller yards did not have their own works and had to buy in engines and boilers from specialist marine engineers, like Rowan's or Dunsmuir & Jackson. Before they were fitted, engines were trial-assembled in the engine works and tested. They were then taken down and re-erected within the hull, along with all the auxiliary machinery such as pumps and windlasses.

The first class cabins and staterooms of passenger liners from about the 1860s were fitted out to very exacting specifications in different styles, depending on the owner's taste. There were Tudor half-timbered dining saloons, Classical ballrooms and plush Empire-style libraries. All the fittings were made by cabinet-makers in the yards and the furnishings were supplied by outside contractors, mostly located in the west of Scotland. The Glasgow carpet-makers, J & J Templeton, wove as many specialist carpets for liners as they did for private homes. Wylie & Lochhead,

Glasgow cabinet-makers, made whole suites of furniture for large ships. All the liner-building yards had extensive joiners' shops and cabinet-making works and some employed gilders and decorators to make wall-coverings and other finishings. One of the difficulties of fitting the interiors of a large ship was the impossibility of hanging a plumb line, which meant that everything had to be carefully measured from the drawings. Until the building of the *Queen Mary* in the 1930s, designers believed that commercial work for the shipyards was beneath their dignity and did not wish their names to be associated with these schemes. However, the surviving records of the shipyards and specialist suppliers make it clear that many well-known artists and architects were commissioned to design interiors for ships.

Not all the accommodation on a liner was for first-class passengers, but even the steerage class, used by emigrants, required vast amounts of furnishings – tables, chairs, bunks and sanitary items. Smaller passenger vessels, like the paddle steamers that plied the waters of the Clyde until the 1950s, were handsomely appointed with rich upholstery and sumptuous table ware. Cargo ships also had cabins and quarters for officers and crew. The master's cabin, where the owner's business was transacted, was usually well equipped. By the end of the 19th century, the expansion of the Clyde shipbuilding industry had caused an enormous number of specialist suppliers to be established in the west of Scotland. Some firms, like the pottery company Royal Doulton, opened works in Glasgow in order to take advantage of the shipbuilding market.

Not all the fitting-out was inside the hull. The decks had to be completed, usually with teak planking imported from Burma and left to season in timber ponds lower down the Clyde. Funnels and ventilators for the enginerooms and lower decks had to be made and fitted. Life-boats and their davits had to be installed, masts erected and the ship rigged. Finally, the whole ship had to be painted in the livery of the owner. When work was finally completed, which, for a large liner, could be as much as a year after the launch, the ship was ready to go on its trials.

The fitting-out of naval vessels was perhaps the most complex task in the whole industry by the end of the 19th century. Apart from the work involved in a commercial contract, a naval vessel had to be armed and battleships protected with armour plating. Fitting a gun turret and the ammunition hoists required specialist contractors as the turret had to be able to swing freely around 180 degrees. The guns and turrets were made by armaments companies like William Beardmore and Co of Parkhead and the Coventry Ordinance Works, which had a plant in Scotstoun and was owned by John Brown's, Fairfield's and Cammell Laird's of Liverpool. The Admiralty were also exacting and infuriating customers, endlessly interfering and changing designs at the last moment. As a result, only a small number of Clyde yards undertook Admiralty work.

The *Princess Maud*, a coastal tramp steamer, built by Napier & Miller for M Langland & Son, under tow to the fitting-out bay after her launch from the Yoker Yard of Napier & Miller in 1901. Langlands were a Liverpool and Glasgow firm of shipowners, with a fleet of ten tramp steamers at the turn of the century.

The magnificent engine works of William Beardmore's new Naval Construction Works at Dalmuir in 1906. This was the largest engine shop on the Clyde and included in the centre a smaller finishing shop for brass work. Although it contained better machine tools than most yards, crucially it was not equipped to manufacture marine turbines.

Lowering the turntable for 'Y' barbette into position on board HMS *Barham* in 1914. The turntables and gun mountings were very complex installations, which were manufactured by specialist munitions companies.

Placing the main armament in position in 'Y' barbette on the Repulse class battleship HMS *Repulse* in 1916.

The deeply upholstered saloon of the paddle steamer *Greyhound*, completed by J & G Thomson in 1895 for the North Pier Steam Packet Co of Blackpool, which operated services to the Mersey ports. All the cabinetwork and upholstery was undertaken in the yard, and the chairs and carpet supplied by local firms.

A paddle steamer in Tod & McGregor's graving dock at their Meadowside yard in the 1860s. Tod & McGregor were unusual in having their own graving dock built in the mid-1850s. For hull inspections, most shipbuilders used the graving docks operated by the Clyde Navigation Trust at Cessnock in Glasgow and the Greenock Harbour Trust in Greenock.

The beautiful gilded paddle box of the *Gwalia*, built by John Brown's for Barry & Bristol Channel Steam Ship Co in 1905. The company, which was managed by W T Symonds & Co of Cardiff, owned three steamers for its Bristol Channel services. Paddle boxes were the most richly decorated external ship fittings, long after figureheads and stern posts had ceased to be ornamented.

The talisman is seen receiving her first coat of British Rail 'buff' at the time of railway nationalisation. The ship was much modified after her wartime service, when the two lifeboats were moved aft of the wheel house and the Welin davits fitted, as can be seen in the photograph.

The funnels of the *Queen Elizabeth* glowing in the Cunard livery after the liner's refit following her war service as a troopship. In the last days of crossing the Atlantic by sea, the *Queen Elizabeth* was enormously popular, partly because so many GIs had come to Europe on her during the war.

THE ACCEPTANCE TRIAL

When a ship was finished, all the working parts had to be tested to ensure that they worked according to specification. Normally the shipyard would conduct its own trials, beginning with dockyard tests and then taking the ship to sea to try out the engine's performance. After these had been completed, the new owners conducted their own trials, in the presence of the builders. For a large passenger liner these could take several days and if, a ship failed to meet requirements, the owners could either refuse to take delivery or negotiate a refund of the price. The most spectacular part of any trial was steaming along the measured mile to gauge the maximum speed of a ship. There were two measured miles on the Clyde – one off Arran and the other off Skelmorlie, on the Ayrshire coast. After the completion of the trials and the correction of any faults, the owner would take delivery, following an inspection of the hull in a dry dock to ensure no damage had been sustained during launching.

In most cases, the ship left the Clyde for her maiden voyage with the owner's crew on board, never to return except for essential repairs. Many large passenger liners took distinguished guests on an acceptance cruise before entering service. Smaller vessels that were not intended to be ocean-going were difficult to deliver. Some were shipped as deck cargo, others had to be taken to pieces and packed in crates, while others had to be rigged as sailing ships and sailed to their destinations – for example, torpedo boat destroyers with powerful but only short-range engines.

After a ship had left, the builder did not destroy the records relating to its construction, as repairing and refitting were lucrative. Until the late 1870s a good deal of maintenance was carried out at sea but, as ships became larger and more sophisticated, more and more maintenance had to be carried out at shipyards. Some builders, like Harland & Wolff of Belfast, made it a condition of their contracts that they had to undertake all repair work.

The *Queen Elizabeth 2*, the last Atlantic liner to be built on the Clyde, being fitted out at John Brown's Clydebank yard in 1968. Despite her modern profile, she was very much in the tradition of the other *Queens* constructed at the yard.

Testing the torpedo tubes on the destroyer HMS *Medea* in 1915. Although weapons were supplied by outside contractors, they had to be tested along with all the other equipment at the time of the trials.

The *Queen Mary* leaving Clydebank on her maiden voyage in 1936.

A last swab of the deck of the cruiser HMS *Bermuda*, before she left for action from the Clydebank yard in 1941. Naval craft were always commissioned from the builder's yard. Even before the keel was laid senior members of the crew were appointed to oversee the construction. As the new ship neared completion, more and more of the crew joined the ship until, by the time of the acceptance trials, the whole complement were on board.

The crew lining the deck of the camouflaged Fiji class cruiser HMS *Bermuda* as she left the Clyde in 1941. She was armed with twelve six-inch and eight five-inch guns. HMS *Bermuda* served in the Home Fleet from 1942–45, and then in the Far East.

THE SHIPYARD PHOTOGRAPHER

Since earliest times, ships have been regarded as objects of beauty. Artists have painted them and exquisite models have been made of them. From the beginning of photography, pictures were taken of ships, normally after they had been completed. When photography became popular and less expensive in the 1880s, the larger shipyards began either to employ their own photographers or to use commercial photographers to record the vessels that they had built. Big yards, like J & G Thomson of Clydebank (later John Brown's) and William Denny and Bros of Dumbarton, set up elaborate photographic departments, which recorded progress at every stage of construction. These photographs seem to have been sent to the customers to show how work was progressing, particularly if a progress payment was due to be made, when work had reached a certain stage. Most yards, however, used commercial photographers, like W & R Ralston of Glasgow, Bale's of Liverpool and Adamson and Robertson of Gourock and Rothesay, to take launch groups, trial shots and, occasionally, sets of interior photographs at the time of delivery. The heyday of ship photography was in the twenty years before the First World War. The photographers used large format 15"x12" or 12"x10"glass negatives, which produced pictures of incredible clarity and depth of field. They became expert in capturing evocative shots of new ships with just the right amount of smoke billowing from the funnel. They also photographed workshops and engines under construction, usually for use in trade publications.

Photography continued during the First World War but, when the recession began to bite in the 1920s, many yards stopped taking pictures. During the Second World War, security was far tighter than in the previous contest and any pictures that were taken had to be sent to the Admiralty or to the Ministry of Shipping. With the advent of smaller cameras and celluloid film, the quality of shipyard photography, like most commercial photography, deteriorated. This was perhaps a reflection of the changing popular perception of heavy engineering and shipbuilding away from being romantic enterprises – the foundations of the Empire – to being dirty unpleasant industries that had little future in the modern world dominated by the motor car. John Brown's was the only Clyde shipyard still to have a photographic department up till the moment the yard ceased to build ships, after the collapse of Upper Clyde Shipbuilders in 1971.

The surviving photographs of the Clyde shipbuilding industry are now housed in archives, libraries and museums - the Archives and Business Record Centre at the University of Glasgow, Glasgow City Council Archives, the National Maritime Museum at Greenwich and the Scottish Maritime Museum at Irvine. They never fail to awe and inspire.

Self-evidently, photographs of photographers are uncommon. Here, a photographer takes a picture of the platform party at a launch from Napier & Miller's yard at Old Kilpatrick in 1911. The camera is housed in the large wooden box on top of the tripod. The sheer size and weight of 19th-century cameras is awesome and is itself testimony to the skill and enterprise of photographers before the First World War.

IMAGES OF SHIPBUILDING

One of the earliest photographs of a Clyde shipyard - the monitor HMS *Erebus* on the stocks at the Govan yard of Robert Napier & Sons in 1856. This was the first armoured vessel to be built on the Clyde. The 4-inch armoured plate was bolted on to a six-inch-thick teak underskin. Napier's undertook to build the ship in four months, employing sometimes as many as 1,200 men at once on the contract. HMS *Erebus* was laid down at the beginning of the year, was launched on 19 April and sailed for Spithead the next day. However the Crimean War came to an end before she had time to steam up the Baltic to shell St Petersburg.

Robert Napier with his foremen and their families in the late 1850s. David Elder, his senior manager and right hand man, is on the right. Most of Napier's foremen from this period went on to establish their own shipyards and engineering businesses. They included Charles Randolph and John Elder, David's son, who established the marine engineering and shipbuilding firm of Randolph & Elder; the brothers James and George Thomson, whose firm J & G Thomson gave the name of their foundry to the new town of Clydebank on the lower Clyde, and Peter Denny, for many years senior partner of William Denny & Bros of Dumbarton. Although his later years were marred by disagreements with his eldest son James R Napier, at the peak of his powers, when this photograph was taken, Robert Napier was widely recognised as the father of Clyde shipbuilding.

WRECK OF THE S.S. MOUNTAINEER . 13837 JV

Who took the plug out? *Mountaineer (1)*, built by James & George Thomson at their Govan yard in 1852, stranded on rocks off the south tip of Lismore in September 1889. She was bound for Oban. As a result of her grounding she broke her back and was lost. This photograph was taken by the well known Dundee firm of Valentines.

The Indian Government's troopship HMS *Malabar*, alongside the Lancefield works of Robert Napier & Sons in 1867. The ship, which was designed by Edward J Reid, the Chief Constructor of the Navy, would have been assisted by sail on long voyages. St Vincent Crescent, one of Glasgow's finest rows of tenements, can be seen in the background. It is easy to forget that the very existence of the British Empire demanded reliable shipping service to every part of the world to transport officials, businessmen and, in this case, troops. Passage to the many parts of the Empire was normally by passenger liner, even in times of emergency, but troops were moved around the coast of India by Government troopship.

The men who made the compound engine – Charles Randolph and John Elder, with their managers and foremen, in the 1860s. Randolph, Elder & Co was the most significant partnership to emerge from Robert Napier's kindergarten. Together they pioneered the marine compound engine and were probably responsible for the Clyde retaining its hegemony in world shipbuilding in the middle decades of the 19th century. Unlike some of their competitors they were astute businessmen, carefully patenting all their innovations and ruthlessly pursuing those who infringed their patents. After his retirement from the firm in the mid-1860s Charles Randolph chaired the Clyde Navigation Trust, putting a great deal of effort into further deepening the river to enable larger vessels to be built on its upper reaches.

The three-masted barque *Margaret Galbraith*, built by Robert Duncan & Sons of Port Glasgow in 1868 – the stock-in-trade of many builders on the lower Clyde until the 1890s. The *Margaret Galbraith* was owned by Paddy Henderson & Co of Glasgow and was employed on their Clyde-Rangoon service. Scots had extensive interests in Burma, particularly in the trade in teak, which was used extensively in shipbuilding. The Margaret Galbraith was immensely seaworthy, reputedly keeping her decks dry even in the roughest conditions. As a result she was popular with her crew, who signed on for voyage after voyage. She was typical of the hundreds of iron sailing ships built on the Clyde in the second half of the 19th century.

The cruiser HMS *Northampton* on the ways at Robert Napier & Sons' Govan yard in 1876. The stern poppets supporting the propeller tubes are clearly visible. This was the last vessel to be ordered from the original firm of Robert Napier & Sons. Robert Napier died at Shandon, his home on the Gareloch, in October 1875. The following year, the firm was taken over by Dr A C Kirk and the brothers John and James Hamilton. James R Napier, who had fallen out with his father, set up his own shipbuilding firm of Napier, Shanks & Bell, with a yard further downstream at Yoker in 1877. Looking back on life in the Govan yard under Robert Napier, Sir William Pearce, then of Fairfield's, commented that the watchword of the yard had always been 'Good Work – and such questions as What time will this take? or What will this cost? were always subordinated to the crucial one – Is this the best?'

Monas Isle was built by Tod & McGregor at their Meadowside yard for the Isle of Man Steam Packet Company's Liverpool to Isle of Man service in 1860. Tod & McGregor were the first shipbuilding company on the Clyde to build ships from iron. Vessels for the Isle of Man services had to be very robust to weather the storms and turbulent waters of the Irish Sea.

One of the most sumptuous interiors produced on the Clyde in the 19th century – the Grand Saloon of the Russian Imperial yacht *Livadia*, built by John Elder & Co in 1885. The yacht had an unusual circular hull, partly to provide protection against underwater explosions, since the Tzar and his family were in constant danger of assassination. Conceived by Admiral Popoff, the lines of the *Livadia* were determined by Dr Tidemann and based on model experiments in Copenhagen after Sir William Pearce, the managing director of the Fairfield yard, had guaranteed a speed of at least 14 knots. Further tests using a small launch were carried out on Loch Lomond to establish the correct pitch and location of the propellers. The *Livadia* was delivered to the Black Sea where she remained largely unused until she was broken up.

The *Grenadier*, built by J & G Thomson in 1885 for David MacBrayne, dis-embarking passengers at Iona. For many years both before and after the First World War, she was employed in the summer months on the Oban–Staffa–Iona route and in the winter on the Gourock–Ardrishaig service. She became enormously popular with the tourists, but although very attractive, her design was outmoded. Her compound oscillating engines were old-fashioned and expensive to run. During the First World War she was converted into a mine-sweeper and renamed HMS *Grenade*. She was burnt out at Oban in 1927 and subsequently broken up.

The Spanish cruiser *Reina Regante* awaiting service at J & G Thomson's Clyde-bank yard in 1887. This was one of the first cruisers to be fitted with a protective deck of 3 to 4 inches thick, which could 'resist the impact of shot and shell from guns of considerable calibre'. Despite this additional weight, the *Reina Regante* had sufficient power to cruise at over 20 knots.

The colossal stern post of the liner *City of New York* after trial assembly in the engine works at Clydebank. The huge steel castings had to be bored and machined to take the stern tubes and the rudder pintle. This liner and her sister ship, the *City of Paris*, were the first successful twin-screw Atlantic liners and the first liners that could make the crossing without the aid of sail. In 1890, in a celebrated accident, the starboard propeller shaft of the *City of Paris* snapped, leaving the liner powerless 200 miles off the coast of Ireland. The cause was never established but suspicion rested on the difficulty of synchronising the engines in early twin screw vessels of this size.

A beautiful photograph of the *City of New York*, built by J & G Thomson for the Inman Line, passing Bowling on her way to sea in 1888. With her sister liner, the *City of Paris*, she was considered to be one of the most handsome and comfortable liners of the late 19th century. Together they were the largest ships then afloat, but not quite as fast as their White Star rivals *Teutonic* and *Majestic*. In a famous race in the autumn of 1890 the *Teutonic* beat the *City of New York* by just five minutes westwards and twelve minutes eastwards.

The well-appointed library of the *City of New York*, 1888. The two Inman liners built by J & G Thomson's set new standards in interior decor. A contemporary commented, 'The introduction of these splendid ships to the Express Transatlantic Service marks one of these epochs of complete transformation in type of vessel, which, as the years roll by, the demands of the public necessitate and advance of engineering science renders possible.' Both liners continued in service until 1923.

The handsome little coaster *Sea Gull*, built by Murdoch & Murray, one of the smaller Clyde yards, in 1892. Steam coasters such as this replaced traditional coastal sailing vessels in the 20 years before the First World War. They were more reliable, could carry larger cargoes, and could get perishable foodstuffs, which made up a large proportion of coastwise trade, to market faster. It is vessels like the *Sea Gull* that John Masefield characterised in his memorable line 'Dirty British coaster with a salt-caked smoke stack'.

The paddle steamer *Glen Sannox*, one of the most beautiful Clyde steamers, built for the Glasgow & South Western Railway Co by J & G Thomson in 1892. She was used almost exclusively on the service between Ardrossan and Arran.

The liners *Danube, Kensington, Moore* and *Slieve Bearnagh* crowding the fitting-out basin at the Clydebank yard in 1893. The *Danube* and her sister ship, the *Nile*, also built by Thomson's, were for the Royal Mail Steam Packet Co's South American service. The *Kensington* and her sister ship, the *Southwark*, built by William Denny & Bros of Dumbarton, were for the American Line and were employed on their London–Philadelphia service. The *Slieve Bearnagh* and her sister ship *Slieve Donard*, also built by Thomson's, were for the Belfast & County Down Railway Co's Irish Sea services. The *Moor* had been built at Clydebank in 1881 for the Union Steam Ship Co's South African routes. More than anything else, this photograph illustrates the versatility and the sheer size of the biggest Clyde yards at the end of the century.

Forging a jacket for a 12-inch naval gun on the 4,000-ton press installed at William Beardmore's Parkhead works in 1894. Forging a gun jacket of this size required immense precision and great care in manipulating the workpiece. In order to direct which way it was to be moved, the forgemaster would cry 'Awa' Parkhead' or 'Awa' Camlachie' (nearby villages). Tradition has it that when the Japanese came to learn the craft of heavy forging at the Beardmore works at about this time, they believed the cries to be intrinsic to the process and adopted them when they later opened their own forges. This huge press was part of a gigantic investment programme initiated by William Beardmore II (later Lord Invernairn) to keep the Parkhead works competitive with the larger English steelmakers and forgemasters – Armstrong Whitworth, Vickers, and John Brown's.

Putting the finishing touches to the captain's gallery on the cruiser HMS Terrible at the Clydebank yard in 1895. The captain's cabin was traditionally in the stern of a naval ship – a left-over from the days of sail. Nevertheless the Terrible was of an advanced design with a highly curved four-inch-thick protective deck and powerful engines. The two nine-inch guns were 'mounted in barbettes and protected by armoured shields of dome shape revolving with the gun'.

A typical Clyde-built cargo ship, the *Clan Chisholm*, constructed for the Clan Line by Alexander Stephen & Sons of Linthouse in 1896. This was one of five new steamers ordered by the company in 1896, when Charles Cayzer was at the peak of his power. The Clan Line had been established in 1878 with the assistance of Alexander Stephen himself, who built Cayzer's first three steamers. Hundreds of vessels like this were built on the Clyde in the 20 years before the First World War and traded in every part of the world.

The fitting-out basin at Fairfield's yard in 1898, with HMS *Hermes* and *Argonaut*, the *Carisbrooke Castle*, the sailing ship *Regele Carol I* and the steam yacht *Atmah*. The *Carisbrooke Castle* was for Donald Currie's Castle Line, which provided services from Southampton to Cape Town. Although economic in operation, the vessel rolled heavily in bad weather. The *Regele Carol I* was ordered by the Roumanian State Railways and the *Atmah* was for the fabulously wealthy merchant banker Baron Rothschild. It is worth noticing that, even as late as this, the north side of the river at Merkland had not been developed. In a few years the Clyde Navigation Trust built huge granaries there.

The launch of the *Sanuki Maru* for the NYK (the Japanese Royal Mail Lines) from the yard of Napier Shanks & Bell in 1897. The Napier family built their first vessel for the Japanese, the *Meiji Maru*, in 1874. This ship is now preserved in Tokyo. The *Sanuki Maru* was one of the fleet of 46 ships that took part in the famous evacuation of refugees after the Great Kanto earthquake in 1923, when 140,000 people died.

The *Dunvegan Castle*, built by Fairfield's for Donald Currie's Castle Line on trial in 1896. Donald Currie was a local man, from Greenock, who had been brought up in Belfast, where he worked for some time as a hairdresser before joing Cunard as a shipping clerk. He left in 1863 to set up his own firm trading with South Africa. He was very successful, not just as a shipowner, but as a shrewd investor in southern Africa's rapidly expanding gold and diamond mines.

The Russian troopship *Moskva*, with the Imperial Eagle at the prow, ready for launch in 1898. The simple launching platform is in the foreground and the drag chains to slow the vessel's passage into the water can be seen by the piles of wooden scaffolding.

The sumptuous saloon of W A Donaldson's steam yacht *Sheelah I*, built by J & G Thomson in 1898. Steam yachts were the most exquisitely fitted of all the ships built on the Clyde. By this time, W A Donaldson, a Glasgow iron merchant, effectively controlled the Clydebank yard. He had bailed the Thomsons out in the early 1890s and, in 1897, had established the Clydebank Engineering & Shipbuilding Co, with himself as Chairman. He later sold out to John Brown's.

The cluttered deck of the Cressy-class cruiser HMS *Sutlej* on trial in 1899. Dockyard workmen are always present during trials. The *Sutlej* carried 700 men. Until the days of wireless, the rigging of naval vessels was elaborate, as it was used to hoist signals.

The bucket dredger *Maru No 2*, built by Lobnitz & Co for Japanese owners in 1900. Lobnitz developed close links with Japan after the Meiji restoration in the 1870s and supplied the first vessel to the NYK (the Japanese Royal Mail Lines). Several Japanese apprentices were trained in the yard and book-keepers from Lobnitz helped to introduce a modern accounting system at Mitsubishi.

One of the most spectacular photographs of Clyde shipbuilding – taken in 1901, a view of the neighbouring Renfrew yards of William Simons & Co and Lobnitz & Co, both specialist dredger builders. There are ten vessels on the ways in the two yards. At this time, most ports throughout the world were up river and could only be kept accessible to large vessels by constant dredging and the removal of spoil far down the estuaries. The Renfrew Ferry can be glimpsed in the far distance.

The Drake-class cruiser HMS *Leviathan* leaving the Clyde, assisted by tugs, in 1901. She carried a complement of 824 men and was armed with 9.2-inch guns. During the First World War, she served on convoy duty as she was too old for front line service. Manoeuvring vessels in the narrow channel of the Clyde was always a difficult task, with the ever-present danger of grounding on a falling tide.

The cargo liner *Italia*, was built in 1904 by Napier & Miller for F C Svorno of Mariupol, Russia.

The cast-steel rudder for the Imperial Russian cruiser *Rurik* at the Parkhead works of William Beardmore & Co in 1905. The *Rurik* was built by Vickers at Barrow and, following Vicker's takeover of William Beardmore & Co, was completed at Beardmore's Dalmuir yard in 1906. She was armed with four ten-inch and eight eight-inch guns, and carried 800 men.

The gun factory at William Beardmore's Parkhead works, opened about 1905. The large machine tool in the foreground was used for trepanning or boring the barrels of the longest naval gun. The steel supports for the building had to be very strong, capable of taking the weight of the overhead crane used for moving and positioning the heavy workpieces.

The imposing *art nouveau* interior of the German liner *Fürst Bismarck*, built by Fairfield's in 1905 for the Hamburg Amerika Line. Shortly afterwards, the German Government prevented contracts for German mail steamers being placed with foreign yards. Interiors such as this were designed by the leading architects of the period, who rarely acknowledged their work in public.

The gantry over the main building berth at William Beardmore's new Dalmuir Naval Construction Works in 1906. The frames and plates were delivered to the gantry by rails from the shops in the background. Unfortunately, the gantry was too low to accommodate the larger dreadnought battleships and battle cruisers built before and during the First World War.

The steam tug *Vigilant* with the steam yacht *Gael* alongside in Lobnitz & Co's fitting-out basin in 1906. A large number of steam yachts for the well-to-do were built on the Clyde between 1890 and 1914 and could be seen in the summer months up and down the west coast. The tripod on the right is a sheerlegs, used for lifting heavy loads on to a vessel during the fitting-out.

The Uruguayan steam tug *Atlantico*, built by Scott's of Bowling for A D & M Lussich, on trial in 1906. The Clyde built many steam tugs during the 19th century for estuarial navigations around the world.

Napier & Miller's new shipyard at Old Kilpatrick in 1906. Even then, in most smaller yards, there was very little in the way of heavy lifting equipment to service the building berths. The firm was reconstructed from Napier, Shanks & Bell by Henry Napier and George Miller as a limited company in 1898. It was forced to move from Yoker in 1906 because the yard was required for the construction of the Rothesay Dock.

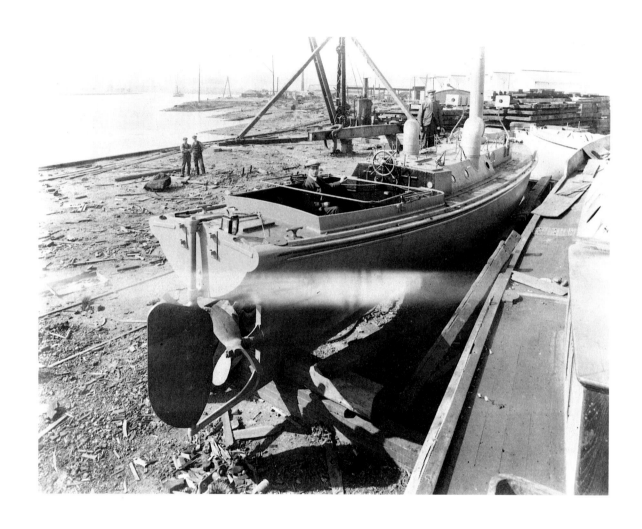

The delightful Captain's steam pinnace from the battle cruiser HMS *Inflexible*, 1907. There were a number of small yards on the river that specialised in such craft, notably Meechan's Scotstoun Iron Works, which specialised in the construction of lifeboats.

The Cunard liner *Lusitania* on trial in 1907, built on the Clyde to compete with the Harland & Wolff giant White Star liners. This ship and her sister, the *Mauretania*, built on the Tyne, dominated the Atlantic in the eight years before the outbreak of war. On her second voyage, the *Lusitania* broke the speed record but was soon overtaken by her sister ship. The *Lusitania* was torpedoed off the Irish coast in May 1915 and sank in under 20 minutes, with the loss of almost 1,200 passengers and crew.

The superb dragon prow of the steam yacht *Sapphire*, built by John Brown's for the Duke of Bedford in 1912.

The launch of the K class destroyer HMS *Acasta* from John Brown's west yard in 1912.

The gunboats HMS *Gnat* and HMS *Myrtle* in the fitting-out basin at Lobnitz & Co's Renfrew yard in 1915. Until the outbreak of the First World War, Lobnitz had not built for the Admiralty, but their expertise in building shallow-draught craft for estuarial navigations made them ideally suited to design and build gunboats.

The fitting-out basin at Clydebank with the Queen Elizabeth class dreadnought HMS *Barham* and three destroyers in 1915. The *Barham* was struck by three torpedoes from U331 on 25 November 1941. Her magazine exploded and she sank quickly with the loss of two thirds of her crew.

Shipyard photographers often wished to present a picture of tidy and orderly construction. This view of the fitting-out basin of John Brown's Clydebank yard illustrates both the confusion and the complexity of shipbuilding. Four vessels, including the cruiser HMS *Canterbury* (left) and the battleship *Barham* (right), were being completed at the yard in 1915. At this time, John Brown's were working round the clock to finish contracts for the Admiralty.

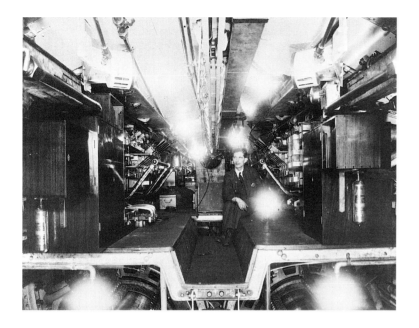

The very cramped engine room of an E class submarine, 1915. The E class was the principal submarine used during the First World War to attack the shipping of Germany and her allies.

A memorable meeting in St Andrew's Hall in Glasgow on 26 December 1915, when Lloyd George, seated in the middle, delivered an impassioned speech to shipyard and munitions workers in an effort to persuade them to accept the dilution of skills during the war. The meeting broke up in confusion and, shortly afterwards, the Government imposed dilution compulsorily

A woman 'dilutee' sitting down to operate a steam hammer during the First World War at the Linthouse yard of Alexander Stephen & Sons. Most yards employed women and unskilled men between 1916 and 1918, because so many able-bodied men had been called up.

One important test before a ship goes to sea for the first time is an inclining experiment, to check that a ship will right herself in heavy seas or, in the case of a naval vessel, after firing a broadside. This experiment shows the cruiser HMS *Tiger* which, although launched in October 1945, was not completed until the next decade.

51. The standard oil tanker *War Hermit*, heavily camouflaged, leaving for war service in 1918. The Professor of Zoology at the University of Glasgow, Sir John Graham Kerr, and the well-known Glasgow artist, Muirhead Bone, helped design the camouflage, which was intended to confuse U boat commanders. Standard ships such as this were built under the authority of the Director of Merchant Shipbuilding, Lord Pirrie (the Chairman of Harland & Wolff) and his Comptroller Sir James Lithgow of the lower Clyde yard of Russell & Co.

Shipyard workers streaming off HMS *Hood* at 5.15 at the end of a day's work in 1919. At this time, shipyard workers often began work at 6.00 in the morning and worked a six-day week, stopping at lunchtime on a Saturday.

The battlecruiser HMS *Repulse* was completed at John Brown's Clydebank yard in 1916. She was sent to Singapore with the battleship *Prince of Wales* in 1941 to provide a 'vague menace'. Without adequate air cover, both ships were sunk by Japanese bombers on 10 December 1941.

The freighter *Waipiata*, built in 1926 for the Union Steam Ship Co of New Zealand by Napier & Miller. In the 1920s, many builders moved the engine room to the stern of cargo vessels to create more space.

Real period pieces of the last days of the Empire – La Salle Jacques Cartier and the Cathay Lounge on the *Empress of Britain*, 1931. Widely admired, she quickly became popular with Canadian passengers. Converted to a troopship, she was bombed off the Aran Islands in 1940 and subsequently torpedoed.

The Clyde paddle steamer *Kenilworth* on the patent slip at A & J Inglis' Pointhouse yard in the 1930s. Patent slips of this type were one of Robert Napier's many inventions. The *Kenilworth* was built by A & J Inglis in 1898 for the North British Railway Co and used on the Rothesay route.

The day's work was suspended on the hull of the giant Cunarder, Ship No 534, at John Brown's yard on 10 December 1931. The abandoned hull became a symbol of the worldwide slump, a constant reminder to the people of Britain and the world of the seriousness of the economic crisis. After long and protracted negotiations, leading to the amalgamation of the Cunard and White Star lines, work resumed in April 1934, signalling the end of the slump. The jubilant workforce were led back into the yard by pipers playing the call to arms.

Resplendent Ship No 534, the *Queen Mary*, awaits the moment of departure from the Clydebank yard in 1936. This magnificent liner, with a sister ship, was intended to provide Cunard's main North Atlantic service. Over the next three years, she vied with the French *Normandie* for the Blue Riband.

The powerful skeleton of Britain's last battleship, HMS *Vanguard*, at Clydebank in 1945.

Camouflaged in battleship grey, the *Queen Elizabeth* leaves Clydebank secretly in February 1940 to be fitted out as a troopship in Singapore. During the war, she carried thousands of GIs across the Atlantic to fight in Europe. She did not enter service with Cunard until after the war, in 1946.

Two views of the crowded berths and fitting-out quay at the Linthouse works of Alexander Stephen & Sons in 1944. The contribution of the Clyde yards during the Second World War was critical, since, except for a few months in the summer of 1941 they were out of range of enemy bombers.

The bakery on the *Queen Elizabeth* when she entered service in 1946. All ships needed galleys, but large liners needed elaborate galleys that could produce a great variety of food, to suit all tastes and classes.

The Illustrious class aircraft carrier *Indefatigable* nearing completion in 1944.

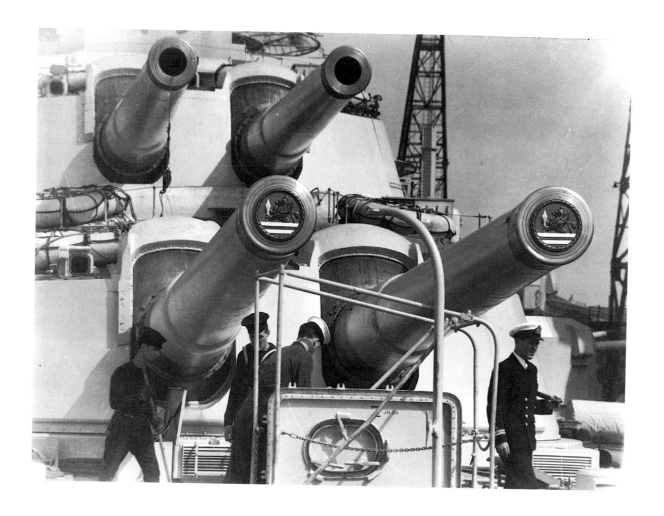

The main armament of the last British battleship HMS *Vanguard*, completed by John Brown's in 1946. The end of large capital ships signalled the end of the integrated armaments industry, which had developed over the previous century. There was no longer any need for steelmasters to own naval shipyards. Weapon systems increasingly became complex electrical installations, where the cost of the hull was largely incidental.

A classic trial view of the oil tanker *Vikfoss*, in 1949. When tankers became larger in the late 1950s, the Clyde was unable to compete for their construction as there were no yards big enough to take them and the Clyde yards were unable to agree to co-operate in the building of a new facility.

Clyde yards, even towards the end of liner building, in the 1950s, could still design imaginative contemporary interiors, as in the winter gardens of the *Olympia*, built for the Trans-Atlantic Shipping Corporation by Alexander Stephen & Sons of Linthouse in 1953.

The *Olympia*, built for the Trans-Atlantic Shipping Corporation by Alexander Stephen & Sons, on trial in 1953.

Lyle Shipping Co's bulk carrier *Cape St Vincent* on trial in 1966. The Lyle Shipping Co was one of Glasgow's last traditional tramp shipping companies.

Lifting the prefabricated bow section into place on the *Samjohn Pioneer*, built by Upper Clyde Shipbuilders in 1972. This photograph represents the belated effort of Clyde shipbuilders to imitate their foreign competitors by introducing production engineering techniques to their yards.

SHIPYARD HISTORIES

BARCLAY CURLE & CO

John Barlcay, the founder of the firm, began shipbuilding at Stobcross Pool on the upper reaches of the Clyde in 1818. His son Robert expanded the business and developed a repair yard. In 1845, the firm was reconstructed as Barclay, Curle & Co, with Robert Barclay, Robert Curle and James Hamilton as partners, diversifying into iron shipbuilding two years later. The firm continued to expand and in 1848, launched one of the largest vessels yet built on the upper river, the *City of Glasgow* weighing 500 tons. In 1855, the firm moved to a larger yard at Whiteinch and, in 1861, an independent engine works was established. Further development of the Whiteinch yard and the creation of a new ship repair business was delayed until 1878 because the Clyde Navigation Trust would not grant permission. The Stobcross yard was closed in 1874 as the site was required for the construction of the new Queen's Dock. From the 1870s, the firm specialised in intermediate cargo liners for the Indian and North American trades. In 1894, the engine works moved to the old premises of J & G Thomson in Finnieston. In 1911, Barclay Curle built the *Jutlandia*, the first ocean-going diesel-engined ship in Britain. The following year, after acquiring the shipbuilding and ship-repairing firm of John Shearer & Sons, with a yard and dry dock at Scotstoun, Barclay Curle itself was taken over by the Tyne shipbuilders Swan Hunter. Together they purchased a controlling interest in the North British Diesel Engine works at Scotstoun, which had been designed by Dr Rudolph Diesel himself. A new yard was laid out towards the end of the First World War and further premises were acquired. Unwanted capacity was closed in 1932. Although shipbuilding stopped in 1967, ship repair continued until 1975 and engine building until 1977 when the plant was converted to the manufacture of weapon systems.

JOHN BROWN SHIPBUILDING & ENGINEERING CO, CLYDEBANK

In the early 20th century this yard came to typify 'Clyde-built' with its series of magnificent Atlantic liners for the Cunard Co, the *Lusitania* (1907), the *Aquitania* (1914), the *Queen Mary* (1936) and the *Queen Elizabeth* (1946). The yard owes its origin and its name to the Clyde Bank Foundry in Anderston in Glasgow, which was established in 1847 by the brothers James and George Thomson, both of whom had worked for Robert Napier. They opened a shipyard at Cessnock Bank in 1851, launching their first ship, the *Jackal*, the following year. Almost immediately, the firm began specialising in high-quality passenger ships, building the *Jura* for Cunard in 1854 and the record-breaking *Russia* in 1867. The yard moved from Cessnock in 1871 to the Barns o' Clyde, rechristened Clydebank after the yard, near the village of Dalmuir. For the next decade, the engine and boiler works remained in Glasgow but, in 1883 and 1884, new works were laid out alongside the shipyard at Clydebank. Although chronically troubled by financial difficulties, the Clydebank yard won an international reputation for quality and innovation. In 1890, the firm became a limited company and control passed to W A Donaldson, a Glasgow iron and steel merchant. The Thomsons, who were themselves heavily in debt, remained on the board until 1897, when they were finally ousted and the company name changed to Clydebank Shipbuilding and Engineering Co. Aware that it would be difficult for the yard to compete without substantial new investments, the directors welcomed an approach from the Sheffield steelmakers John Brown & Co in 1899. Immediately John Brown's embarked on a massive programme of re-equipment, which had cost almost £900,000 by 1914. The accompanying extension and strengthening of the berths and the fitting-out basin allowed the yard to capture the contract for the Cunard liner *Lusitania*. At the same time, recognising the importance of the marine turbine, Brown's purchased the machines required to make and set turbine blades, and also took out a licence for the American Curtis turbine, which was modified for naval use as the Brown-Curtis turbine. John Brown's intention in buying the yard was to secure an outlet for its armour-plate and heavy steel forgings and, as a result, increasingly the order book was dominated by naval vessels, particularly capital ships. During the war, the yard built naval vessels of all types and for every theatre of action. With the collapse of Admiralty work in the 1920s, John Brown's suffered, and the yard was closed between 1931 and 1934, with the half-completed Ship No 534, the *Queen Mary*, on the ways. Prosperity returned during the Second World War and during the short-lived postwar boom. In 1953, John Brown & Co (Clydebank) Ltd was set up to manage the Clydebank works and, in 1966, the engineering business was separated from the shipyard. This was a prelude to the formation of Upper Clyde Shipbuilders in 1968, which failed in 1972. The yard was then sold for oil-rig building and shipbuilding ceased.

CHARLES CONNELL LTD

Charles Connell, the manager of Alexander Stephen & Sons' Kelvinhaugh shipyard, set up his own yard at Scotstoun in 1863, specialising in large tramp sailing ships, notably the tea clipper *Taitsing*. The firm began building passenger vessels, including, in 1883, the *City of Chicago* for the Inman Line, which was always considered to be well below the high standard of other Inman liners. After Charles Connell's death in 1884, the firm was managed by his sons, and remained a family business until the formation of Upper Clyde Shipbuilders in 1968. The yard shut down in 1930 and did not re-open until the depression was over in 1938. After the failure of Upper Clyde Shipbuilders in 1971, the yard was transferred to Scotstoun Marine Ltd, and finally closed in 1980.

William Denny & Bros of Dumbarton

The Denny family has a long association with shipbuilding in the lower Clyde town of Dumbarton, going back to the late 18th century. In 1814, William Denny, the father of the founder of the firm, constructed the *Margery*, the first steamer on the Thames. The firm was established by his sons William Denny II, Alexander, James and Peter as Denny Bros but, after a disagreement, when Alexander left, was reconstituted in 1849 as William Denny & Bros. In 1850, Peter Denny, John McAusland and John Tulloch established the marine engineering firm of Tulloch & Denny, chiefly to build engines for the yard. William Denny II died in 1851 and Peter Denny assumed control. Under his direction the firm established close relations with the Glasgow shipowners Paddy Henderson & Co and their related shipping lines, including the Irrawaddy Flotilla Company and the Albion Line. A new shipyard at Dumbarton, the North yard, was purchased in 1859 and the engine works of Tulloch & Denny was enlarged. On John Tulloch's retirement in 1862, the engine works was renamed Denny & Co and, during the next decade, built the first compound engines for both Cunard and P & O. Peter's eldest son, the talented naval architect William Denny III, became a partner in 1868 and quickly assumed the role of yard manager, making all sorts of improvements and reforms. He pioneered steel shipbuilding in the *Rotomahana* of 1879, completely reconstructed the yard in 1881, and built the first commercial test tank in the world in 1883. Deeply distressed by the disastrous investment in the South American La Platanese Flotilla Company, William Denny III committed suicide in 1887. Despite this tragic loss, Denny's continued to be pioneers and innovators, building the first turbine passenger steamer, the *King Edward*, in 1901 and the first merchant ship with combined reciprocating and turbine machinery, *Otaki*, for the Henderson-controlled New Zealand Shipping Company in 1908. The shipyard and engine works were merged in 1918. After an unsuccessful attempt to build hovercraft, the firm went into liquidation in 1963.

Fairfield Shipbuilding & Engineering Co, Govan

The works of Fairfield Shipbuilding & Engineering Co is the only large merchant shipbuilding yard to survive on the upper reaches of the river. The firm began marine engineering when John Elder became a partner in the millwrighting business of Randolph Elliot & Co, with works in Centre Street, Glasgow. Under the name Randolph Elder & Co, Charles Randolph and John Elder invented and developed the marine compound engine, which over the next 20 years became the standard means of propulsion for larger vessels. They began shipbuilding in Govan in 1860 and, in 1864, built a large yard lower down the river at Fairfield. An enormous engine works was added in 1868, and production concentrated at Govan. Charles Randolph retired in that year and the firm's name was changed to John

Elder & Co. The following year, John Elder died of cancer and a new partnership formed, headed by William Pearce, the general manager of Robert Napier's shipyard. Under his able direction the firm became one of the most important shipbuilders in the world, constructing a series of 'greyhounds of the Atlantic', including the *Umbria* and the *Etruria* (1884-85) for Cunard & Co. William Pearce became an MP in 1885 and, so as to allow his firm to compete for Admiralty contracts, it was converted into a limited company as the Fairfield Shipbuilding & Engineering Co. Pearce, who had been created a baronet, died in 1888 and was succeeded as chairman by his son, Sir W G Pearce. The firm reached its zenith in 1893, with the construction of the *Campania* and the *Lucania* for Cunard; thereafter the size of the berths made it impossible any longer to tender for the largest Atlantic liners. Instead, Fairfield concentrated on long-haul liners for the Canadian and South African trades and, perhaps more importantly, on Admiralty work. Fairfield's became part of Clarence Hatry's ill-fated and fraudulent Northumberland Shipbuilding Group in 1919 and only managed to survive by sacrificing the greater part of its financial reserves. Driven to the verge of bankruptcy, it was rescued by the Bank of England and taken over by Lithgows in 1935. The business was liquidated in 1965 but saved by the Government as Fairfield (Glasgow) Ltd, which, under Iain Stewart's direction, attempted to introduce new working practices. In 1968, the yard passed under the control of Upper Clyde Shipbuilders

and, when that failed in 1972, was once again rescued by the government. Today, the yard is owned by Kvaerner, the Finnish shipbuilding and engineering group.

D & W HENDERSON, MEADOWSIDE

This yard owes its origins to the firm of Tod & McGregor, established by David Tod and John McGregor, two of David Napier's sea-going engineers and, later, foremen. When Napier began to explore the possibility of moving to London in 1833, they opened their own engineering works in Carrick Street, Glasgow. The success of their first marine engines encouraged them to open their own shipyard in 1838, first in Govan, across the river from Napier's Lancefield works and, when this site was required for improving the river in 1844, at Meadowside, at the mouth of the Kelvin. The yard was swamped in a great storm in 1856, the year in which a large new dry dock was opened. In 1872, when Tod & McGregor's sons retired, the business was acquired by Handayside & Henderson, the founders of the Anchor Line. Subsequently, the name was changed to D & W Henderson. The firm was taken over by Harland & Wolff in 1919, and the shipyard closed by National Shipbuilders Security Ltd in 1935. The repair works shut down finally in 1965. Apart from building a large number of liners for Henderson Bros, the family's shipping business, D & W Henderson, also specialised in large yachts, like the *Britannia* for the Prince of Wales in 1893, the *Gleniffer* for James Coats in 1899, and the renowned *Valkyrie III* in 1895.

A & J INGLIS

The brothers Anthony and John Inglis were trained by Tod & McGregor. Anthony began business as a bellhanger, gas-fitter and general engineer in Anderston during 1840. On being joined by his brother John, they started building marine engines and boilers at the Whitehill Foundry in 1847. During the 1850s the firm's reputation for marine engineering grew quickly after the delivery of the engines for the *Tasmania*, one of the fastest ships of the time. They began shipbuilding at Pointhouse, at the mouth of the river Kelvin, opposite Meadowside, in 1862. One of their early ships was the *Erl King*, the first ship to steam to Shanghai around the Cape of Good Hope. The yard built up a close relationship with the Glasgow-based British India Steam Navigation Company, building 53 ships for the line before the First World War. However, the yard was best known for its fast paddlesteamers and handsome steam yachts: the *Safa-el-Bar* for the Khedive of Egypt in 1894 and the *Alexandria* for King Edward VII in 1907. The Pointhouse yard was taken over by Harland & Wolff in 1919 and closed in 1965.

LITHGOW'S LTD, PORT GLASGOW

This business was established as Russell & Co in 1874 by three experienced tramp ship builders: Anderston Rodger, Joseph Russell and William Tod Lithgow at the Bay yard in Port Glasgow. From the outset the firm specialised in large sailing vessels, three- and four-masted barques, the bulk carriers of their day. Lithgow was responsible for the design of the ships, introducing standard features and labour-saving devices, particularly for handling the sails and cargo. The partners won business by offering customers generous financial packages, usually substantial investment in the new ship by themselves and their family and friends. They were instantly successful, expanding in 1879 by acquiring the Cartsdyke yard of J E Scott, who had gone bankrupt, and building a completely new yard at Kingston in 1881. Between 1882 and 1892, the firm built more ships than any other yard on the river - a total of 271 vessels. The original partnership was dissolved in 1891 and Lithgow continued as sole partner in Russell & Co at the Cartsdyke and Kingston yards. Although he had retired, Joseph Russell continued to assist Lithgow in the business. At the turn of the century, he ceased building sailing ships and converted entirely to steam tramps. Knowing he was mortally ill, Lithgow took his young sons James and Henry into partnership in 1907. On his death the following year, with Russell's help they took control of what was one of the most successful merchant shipbuilding enterprises on the river. During the First World War, they enlarged the business by taking over the Port Glasgow yard of Robert Duncan & Co and taking a stake in the Glasgow marine engineers, David Rowan & Co. At the end of the war, the company was renamed Lithgow's Ltd and, in 1919, took over two more Port Glasgow yards, William Hamilton & Co and Dunlop Bremner & Co. Other acquisitions followed including the

Ayrshire Dockyard Co in 1923 and Fairfield's in 1935. The group, with the exemption of Fairfields, continued to specialise in tramp ships and cargo boats. Lithgow's merged with Scott's Shipbuilding & Engineering Co in 1967 and, after nationalisation in 1977, the family withdrew. The business was subsequently taken over by Trafalgar House in 1984 and the yards closed.

LOBNITZ & CO OF RENFREW

In 1847, James Henderson, a member of the Glasgow shipowning family, began shipbuilding at Renfrew. In 1861, the firm became Henderson & Coulborn and followed its new neighbour at Renfrew, William Simons & Co, in specialising in steam tugs, dredgers and associated craft. Henry Lobnitz from Copenhagen became a partner in 1874 and developed close links with Meiji Japan. Lobnitz became sole partner in 1880, after which the business was known as Lobnitz & Co. The business was acquired by Hedmex Investments Ltd in 1957 and was subsequently taken over by G & J Weir, the Glasgow manufacturers of marine pumps, who also now owned the neighbouring yard of William Simons & Co. The two companies were merged as Simons-Lobnitz, which in turn was bought by Alexander Stephen & Sons. The yard was closed in 1964 and all dredger building transferred to Linthouse.

ROBERT NAPIER & SONS, GOVAN

Robert Napier, even in his lifetime, was recognised as the undisputed father of Clyde shipbuilding. He came from a family with a long association with metalworking and engineering in the West of Scotland. Apprenticed in his father's works, where he became skilled in ornamental metalwork and millwrighting, he completed his time in 1812 and went to work in Edinburgh for Robert Stevenson, the lighthouse builder. Moving to the Glasgow works of William Lang in 1814, he set up as a smith on his own the following year. When his cousin, David Napier, moved his marine engineering business to Lancefield, beside the Clyde, on the other side of the city in 1821, Robert took over his Camlachie works, appointing David Elder as his works manager. Wishing to build marine engines like his cousin, he won an order in 1823 for the paddle steamer *Leven*, which is now preserved outside the Denny test tank at Dumbarton. The engines, which incorporated several novel features, outlasted three hulls. Further orders were quickly placed with the firm. In 1827, his skill as an engine builder was confirmed when two steamers fitted with his engines won a race sponsored by the Northern Yacht Club. The race attracted the attention of Thomas Assheton Smith who over the next 20 years ordered a series of innovative steam yachts from Napier. Smith was well connected and gave Napier access to those with influence in London society and in Government. Following this success, Napier purchased the Camlachie works and the Vulcan Foundry, which was not far from the Lancefield works. In 1830, Napier handed over the Camlachie works to one of his brothers and, with

Elder's help, re-equipped the Vulcan Foundry to build large marine engines. Although one of the first contracts of the new shop for the Dundee & Leith Steam Packet Co was beset with difficulty and delay, the engines, when finally delivered, performed so well that they greatly enhanced Napier's reputation. In 1835, he leased the Lancefield works from his cousin David, who was moving to London, and purchased them outright in 1841. From the early 1830s, Robert Napier had been interested in the possibility of setting up a regular and profitable steamship service across the North Atlantic. It was not until Samuel Cunard's British and North American Steam Packet Co. was established in 1839 that he received contracts for an Atlantic steamer and then only after investing in the new company. Over the next 20 years, Napier's built a series of larger and larger liners for Cunard. In 1842, Napier began building his own iron ships at a yard in Govan, on the other side of the Clyde from his Lancefield works; previously, all his hulls had been of wood and constructed by John Wood of Port Glasgow. By the early 1850s, Robert Napier dominated the fast-expanding Clyde marine engineering and shipbuilding industry, attracting a galaxy of able young managers and apprentices, many of whom went on to found or control their own businesses. Renamed Robert Napier & Sons in 1852, the business was left in the day-to-day management of his sons James R Napier, one of the most distinguished marine engineers of his generation, and John Napier. Although orders continued to flow, Napier's began

to lose its technical advantage to competitors on the river such as Thomson's, Elder's and Denny's. The firm's financial position deteriorated, exacerbated by an open disagreement between Robert and his sons about the future direction of the enterprise. By 1871, the Bank of Scotland was unwilling to advance any further money and, on Napier's death five years later, the business was taken over by a partnership consisting of Dr A C Kirk, engine works manager of John Elder & Co, and the brothers John and James Hamilton, Napier's managers. Convinced that the firm's financial difficulties were due to Napier's exacting standards of workmanship, they began to tender for a greater variety of work, and successfully introduced the triple expansion engine, developed by Kirk while he was still at Elder's. Although profitable in the 1880s, the business began to lose money once again in the 1890s and, virtually bankrupt, was acquired by William Beardmore & Co in 1899. In 1905, the yard and engine works were moved down the river to a purpose-built Naval Construction Works at Dalmuir. In building these works, William Beardmore had overstretched himself and was forced to sell out to the armaments group, Vickers. As a result, the new yard never lived up to expectations and was forced out of business during the inter-war depression.

Scott's of Bowling

The Forth and Clyde Canal, which runs from the north shore of the Firth of Clyde at Bowling to Bo'ness on the southern shore of the Firth of Forth, included in its original design a graving dock at Bowling for the repair of vessels using the navigation. In 1800, this was let to Thomas McGill, whose family had for some time been building ships at Port Glasgow and who himself had more recently been repairing gabbarts and wherries at the Broomielaw in Glasgow. McGill constructed his first ship at Bowling in 1804 for Scotts of Dunerbuck. The business prospered and, by 1834, McGill was employing ten journeymen and six apprentice shipwrights. In 1842, he built the *Bowling*, a barque of over 250 tons. When the canal was enlarged the yard was moved to Littlemill in 1851. By then, James Scott had become a partner and the firm's title was changed to Scott & McGill. When Thomas McGill retired in 1867, it became Scott & Sons. Increasingly, the yard specialised in tugs, steam trawlers and small coasters. The yard was taken over by Scott's Shipbuilding & Engineering Co of Greenock in 1965 and closed in 1979.

SCOTT'S SHIPBUILDING & ENGINEERING CO, GREENOCK

Although many of the Clyde yards were without doubt on sites where shipbuilding had been carried on for centuries, and families such as the Dennys has long associations with the trade, Scott's was the shipyard with the longest continuous history of any yard on the river. John Scott began building small fishing boats and coastal craft at Greenock in 1711, a trade which was carried on by successive generations of the family throughout the 18th century. As the Clyde's trade with North America expanded and the War of Independence prevented Glasgow merchants from buying new tonnage there, so Scott's began to build larger ocean-going craft. In the 1790s, the firm launched the *Brunswick*, of 600 tons, and the *Caledonia*, of 650 tons, and, from then on, the family specialised in the construction of large East Indiamen, culminating in the celebrated *Lord of the Isles* of 1853. This clipper, in 1856, beat two of the fastest American ships in a race from Foo-chow to London, delivering her cargo 'without one spot of damage'. There were close links between the Scotts and James Watt's family, who also came from Greenock, resulting in the yard's quick adoption of steam propulsion. By 1816 the Scotts had built two of the earliest Clyde steamers, the *Active* and the *Despatch*, and also the *Shannon* for the service between Limerick and Kilrush. Between 1819 and 1821, the Scotts built the largest steamers in the United Kingdom – the *Waterloo* of 200 tons in 1819, the *Superb* of 240 tons in 1820 and the *Majestic* of 345 tons in 1821. Although the *Superb* was built for the Glasgow–Liverpool trade, she became one of the first steamers to venture into the Mediterranean. The engines of these early steamers were built in Glasgow but, in 1825, the firm bought its own engine works in Greenock, building their first engines for the Mediterranean steamer *Trincania*. By 1829, the engine works was constructing 'the largest engines ever made' and the yard was described as 'the most complete in Britain, excepting those of the Crown'. From then until the 1860s,

Scott's reputation for steamship building was only challenged by Napier's. Scott's market was not for main line Atlantic vessels, but rather for ships for the longer routes to Egypt, India, South Africa and the West Indies. In 1865–66 they built the first three iron steamers, the *Agamemnon*, the *Ajax*, and the *Achilles* for the Holt Line, amongst the first long-distance ships with compound engines. From then until the First World War, Scott's launched, on average, one vessel a year for Holt's and another for the China Steam Navigation Co, owned by the Swires. The yard's association with the Admiralty was the longest on the Clyde, beginning in 1803 with the construction of HMS *Prince of Wales* and continuing with the first steam frigate to be built on the river, HMS *Greenock*. From the 1830s to the 1890s, the majority of the Admiralty work carried out by Scott's was in the development of high-pressure water tube boilers, which were incorporated in two ships, HMS *Thrush* and HMS *Sparrow*, built in 1888 and 1889. From then until the outbreak of the First World War, the yard became increasingly engaged in Admiralty work, engining four battleships and building the dreadnoughts HMS *Colossus* (1909) and HMS *Ajax* (1912). In 1912, the Admiralty ordered 'S1', the first submarine to be built in Scotland, establishing Scott's reputation for submarine building, which continued until the 1970s. The firm's association with Holt's and Swire's carried it through the inter-war years. In 1934, after an exchange of yards with the Greenock Dockyard Co Scott's had a continuous frontage along the shore at Greenock. Scott's merged with Lithgow's in 1967 as Scott Lithgow Ltd and was nationalised in 1977. This business was acquired by Trafalgar House in 1984 and shipbuilding stopped in 1986.

WILLIAM SIMONS & CO, RENFREW

William Simons began shipbuilding at Greenock in 1810, but two years later moved to the Isle Aux Noix, near Montreal, in Canada, where the supply of shipbuilding timber was more plentiful. Here, he built naval vessels for the war of 1812 with the United States. Simons returned to Greenock in 1818 and continued building sailing vessels. He constructed his first steamer, the *Fingal*, for a Belfast company. In 1853, the yard moved to Whiteinch and, in 1860, took over the London Works of Fox Henderson & Co at Renfrew and the adjoining shipyard of J W Hoby & Co. The business passed to the control of Andrew Brown, Simons' partner, and became a limited company in 1895. With the construction of four self-propelling hopper barges for the Clyde Trustees between 1861 and 1863, the firm began its long association with dredger building. Between 1866 and 1872, the yard launched eleven bucket dredgers and nine stationary and propelling dredgers. In 1872, the firm combined the bucket ladder dredger and hopper barge to produce the first hopper dredger, the *Canada*, and in 1889, the first suction dredger, the *Beaver*, for the Natal Government. By 1900, Simons had built over 200 dredgers, improving their original design by introducing the stern wheel dredger and the suction dredger in 1889. In addition, Simons built some other important vessels, including, in 1861, the PS *Rothesay Castle*, which was converted into a blockade runner, and, in 1868, the *India* for the Anchor Line, the first transatlantic liner fitted with four cylinder compound engines. The yard maintained its reputation as dredger builders in the first half of the 20th century. It was taken over by G & J Weir, the Glasgow marine pump manufacturers, in 1957, and was merged with the neighbouring yard of Lobnitz & Co in 1959. Alexander Stephen & Sons acquired Simons Lobnitz in 1959 and the yard closed in 1964.

ALEXANDER STEPHEN & SONS

In 1750, Alexander Stephen began building ships at Burghead, eight miles from Lossiemouth, on the Moray Firth. Alexander's nephew William followed him into business, serving ten years at Burghead before setting up his own yard at Footdee, Aberdeen, in 1793. William's son, another William, also set up his own yard at Arbroath in 1814. Both the Aberdeen and Arbroath yards foundered in 1828 and were taken over by William's eldest son Alexander. From then on, the firm was known as Alexander Stephen & Sons. In 1830, the Aberdeen yard was closed and, in 1843, Alexander moved the centre of his production to the Tay at Dundee. In 1850, the firm built the *Amazon*, of 800 tons, the largest ship built on the river so far. Early the following year, Alexander moved to Kelvinhaugh, on the

Clyde, to begin iron shipbuilding, leaving his son William in charge at Dundee. Stephen's first Clyde-built ship was the *William McCormick*, completed in 1854. In October 1861, Alexander Stephen, the son of the founder of the Kelvinhaugh yard, won approval from the Admiralty and Lloyds to build composite ships with 'bones of iron and skin of wood'. The firm moved to its final home at Linthouse, across the Clyde from Kelvinhaugh, in Govan, during 1869. Until then, the family had specialised in sailing vessels, building the occasional steamship with engines bought in from outside. In 1871, an engine works was built at Linthouse and the yard began to concentrate on cargo-passenger vessels. Stephen's built the first four such steamers for the newly formed Clan Line in 1878–79. By 1886, the family had built 193 ships on the Clyde, 12 more than their nearest rival, Barclay, Curle & Co. The Dundee yard was sold in 1894. The Allan liner *Virginia* was built at Linthouse in 1904, one of the first turbine-driven Atlantic steamers. The *Port Morant* was built in 1901, the first of a succession of banana boats, which included, in 1905, the *Nicaya*, for the newly established firm of Elder & Fyffe's. The firm retained its close relations with the Clan Line and Furness Withy over the next 20 years. The Cayzer family acquired a controlling interest in the business after the First World War but, with the onset of the depression, this relationship proved a burden to both sides and the Stephens regained control. Stephen's took over Simons-Lobnitz, the dredger builders, in 1963 and itself became part of Upper

Clyde Shipbuilders in 1968, when the yard was closed to make way for the Clyde Tunnel.

Yarrow & Co, Scotstoun

Yarrow's was established in 1865 at Folly Wall on the Isle of Dogs in the Thames by Alfred Fernandez Yarrow (1842–1932), a brilliantly gifted engineer. The business started as general engineers but quickly diversified into the construction of steam launches, river boats and other small craft. In 1871, Yarrow became interested in torpedo boats, building his first experimental boat, equipped with a spar torpedo, the following year. By 1877, his reputation for such fast craft was well established. With the development in that year of the self-propelled torpedo, navies around the world came to appreciate the importance of fast manoeuvrable torpedo boats in modern warfare, and orders poured in. Under the direction of Lord Fisher of dreadnought fame, in 1892, Yarrow built HMS *Havock* and HMS *Hornet*, the first destroyers which were designed to chase and, as the name implies, destroy enemy torpedo boats. In 1906, Yarrow decided to leave the Thames and move to a well-established shipbuilding centre. He chose Glasgow and the new yard and engine works on a greenfield site was fully operational within a year. After the boom war years, Yarrow was briefly liquidated, and reconstructed in 1928. The yard remained open throughout the recession. In a successful attempt to corner the market for destroyers, the company, in 1942, set up Yarrow Admiralty Research Department, which continues today as a separate company. Increasingly specialising in torpedo boats and destroyers, the yard expanded to embrace adjoining yards, which were either defunct or on the verge of failure. In 1965, the Blythswood yard of the Blythswood Shipbuilding Co was acquired and, in 1975, the Elderslie dry dock was bought from Barclay Curle. Yarrow's became part of Upper Clyde Shipbuilders but left the group before it collapsed in 1971. Yarrow's became a subsidiary of GEC in 1985.

The author would like to thank Philippa Moss for typing the manuscript, Tom Allison, J M Bennett, John T A Brown, George Gardner and K C Fraser, and the following for permission to reproduce illustrations:

The University of Glasgow Archives and Business Records Centre,
Adamson Robertson collection, pages 48, 49, 93, 99, 104, 114, 123
Alexander Stephen Collection, pages 130 left, 141, 146, 147
Napier Collection, pages 59, 60, 66, 84, 86, 87, 89, 92, 103, 106, 121, 134
William Beardmore collection, pages 39, 41, 47, 67, 102, 115, 116, 118

Keeper of the Records of Scotland
John Brown collection, pages 40, 42, 46, 50–54, 56-58, 61, 62, 68–70, 72, 74, 77–81, 88, 95 *right*, 96-8, 100-1, 108-10, 113, 122, 124, 125, 130 *right*, 131-33, 135,139–40,142–45,148
Fairfield collection, pages 90, 94, 105, 107, 117
Scotts of Bowling, 120
Simons-Lobnitz collection, pages 111, 112, 119, 126–28, 129 left

Sir William Lithgow, page 91